The One-Stock Portfolio

The Simplest Path to Wealth

Heikin Ashi Trader

DAO PRESS

© 2025 Heikin Ashi Trader

Paperback ISBN: 979-8-9928155-8-0

Hardcover ISBN: 979-8-9928155-9-7

Published by Dao Press

an imprint of Splendid Island LLC

Suite 101, 3833 Powerline Road

Fort Lauderdale, FL 33309, USA

Charts by TradingView

First Edition, 2025

Table of Contents

Part 1: Why One Stock Is Enough to Build Wealth

Why We Invest

In my view, there are two main reasons to invest in the stock market. The first might surprise you: it's simply to preserve purchasing power. In this case, you invest in a broadly diversified portfolio—stocks, funds, or ETFs—with the aim of earning a return of around 7 to 8 percent per year. This return roughly offsets the annual loss in purchasing power you would experience by leaving your money in the bank.

Of course, there are also those who don't invest at all and do exactly that: they leave their money in the bank. My uncle Theo is a good example. He's 87, spry and cheerful. Three times a week, he takes the bus into town to eat at his favorite restaurant. His money isn't under the mattress (though I'm not entirely sure), but it's definitely sitting in his bank account. The interest he earns is microscopic. I once tried to explain the principle of systematic monetary devaluation by central banks. He ended the conversation with a simple gesture: he wants nothing to do with it. And he couldn't care less what happens to his money after he's gone. "I sleep like a baby," he says. He'd rather enjoy his money while he still can. He has no heirs, so he has no one to consider. Thankfully, I occasionally benefit from his "investments," since he sometimes invites me to lunch at his beloved restaurant. We laugh heartily over old family stories—and paying the bill is strictly his business. I'm not even allowed to cover the coffee or tiramisu.

There are more "investors" like my uncle Theo than you might think. These people are well aware of the effort and risk that come with real estate or other investments—and they consciously choose not to bother. They've never bought a stock in their life and have no intention of doing so. Their money is always accessible; they are "highly liquid," walking wallets, so to speak.

To be honest, I'm a little envious of these people. They don't worry about stock prices, inflation, or recessions. As long as the money lasts, they enjoy life to the fullest. If a need arises, they have the means to meet it. They don't feel the need to preserve or grow their capital. It's simply enough. This group belongs to the stock market abstainers—and frankly, life's not so bad when you're one of them.

But let's return to the two reasons why one might choose to invest in the stock market anyway. The first group of investors seeks to preserve purchasing power. These people have money and want to invest it in a way that allows them to do or buy the same things ten or twenty years from now that they can today. Their portfolio grows nominally, but in terms of purchasing power, their "wealth" remains about the same. May I say that even achieving this is a considerable accomplishment?

A more ambitious version of this group not only wants to maintain purchasing power but also generate passive income. These investors deliberately choose high-dividend stocks to receive regular payouts. One day, these dividends should supplement or even replace their earned income. Instead of withdrawing money from the bank (or under the mattress), dividends pay the restaurant bills. Uncle Theo would probably just laugh: "If you want to spend money, then just spend it!" he'd likely say. I've given up trying to explain the advantages of a dividend strategy to him. The idea of entrusting his money to some "stranger" or corporation is completely foreign to him. "You'll probably have to pay tax on that payout, too," he'd add—and of course, he's right. It's worth noting that Uncle Theo is no friend of the tax office.

Now we come to the second reason for investing in the stock market: the miracle of wealth creation. This form of investing is relatively young. It did exist in the 17th century during the *tulip mania* in the Netherlands, but only recently has this type of investor become more common: the speculators. This species isn't interested in preserving value but in striking it rich—fast. They are the fortune hunters of the market. It's a rare breed, a late bloomer in evolutionary terms, since the first group—the income seekers and capital preservers—has a much longer and more solid track record.

Speculators have come under heavy fire from the academic community. The wise minds of financial economics agree: it is not possible to consistently beat the market. Markets are so efficient, they say, that at best one might achieve short-term outperformance. But those gains will sooner or later be erased by inevitable losses. Anyone aiming for more than the usual 7 to 8 percent annual return, the experts warn, is defying logic—

at least if you trust their data and statistics. And indeed, their arguments are hard to dismiss. A glance at brokerage account data reveals that many of these ambitious investors can't even keep up with the first group—the steady wealth preservers.

When friends or acquaintances ask me what they should invest in, my answer is always clear: join the first group. Invest your money so that your purchasing power remains intact. Buy good companies or funds that generate a growing stream of dividend income. That's my recommendation. And I don't say that out of theory but from conviction and experience. It's also a strategy that lets you sleep well at night—maybe not quite as soundly as Uncle Theo, but certainly better than most speculators who lose sleep every time the market dips. In fact, for dividend investors, falling prices are a gift—but I've explained that in detail elsewhere (in my book *Stocks are Fun!*).

Even though this investment style is sensible and easy for beginners to learn, hardly anyone follows my advice. Almost no one does it—not even people with considerable financial resources. Young investors don't either. I try to explain that, because of their long investment horizon, they have a huge advantage. If they started a dividend strategy now, even with modest funds, they could build an income stream within 20 or 25 years that would make working optional. They could dine at the finest restaurants every day—not just three times a week like Uncle Theo. I show them how easily this can be achieved with patience and persistence. But they don't listen. To their ears, a 7 or 8 percent return sounds ridiculous. Not even worth considering—even when you factor in the compound interest effect over time.

They're convinced they belong to the chosen few who will not just beat the market but crush it. As you can see, everyone wants to be in the second group. These days, everyone wants to be a speculator, a treasure hunter. And it is for this group that I'm writing this book. Because if you're going to aim high, you should at least know how to significantly improve your odds. Maybe you'll even listen to someone who has already walked this path—like me. I too once thought an 8 percent annual return was laughably low. Of course, I wanted more.

If you want to beat the market, you have to do something different from the market. If you're content with market-level returns, you can simply buy an index ETF. Such funds track the entire market and keep buying regardless of price fluctuations. This means you hold both the stars—Apple, Amazon, Tesla, and others—as well as the laggards that drag down the index. You're not doing anything wrong—but you're not doing anything especially right either. At best, you preserve your purchasing power and grow slowly. There's nothing wrong with that—anyone who invests consistently in an index ETF over 30 years is achieving something remarkable. The sheer discipline to stay the course deserves admiration.

But there's something you should know: the more stocks you hold in your portfolio, the more your performance will mirror that of the overall market. With a bit of investment experience, you'll notice it yourself: some of your stocks do great, others disappoint. A few beat the index—many drag your returns down. And here's the dilemma: diversification reduces risk—but only up to a point. Studies have shown that a portfolio with just ten different stocks is already sufficiently diversified. You don't need fifty or a hundred holdings to have a balanced portfolio.

One of the most commonly repeated pieces of investment advice is also one of the most misunderstood: "Don't put all your eggs in one basket." It sounds reasonable. It feels safe. And because it's so often repeated—especially to beginners—it rarely gets questioned. But for those who want to do more than just preserve wealth, for those who want to build real wealth, this advice becomes a serious obstacle.

So what does diversification really mean? Quite simply, it means spreading your capital across many different investments—different stocks, industries, countries, and ideally across multiple asset classes like bonds, real estate, or commodities. The goal is to reduce risk. The theory behind it is elegant: if one investment performs poorly, another one will compensate for the loss. This supposedly creates a stable, resilient portfolio. In traditional finance, this idea has practically achieved the status of dogma.

But here's the key point: diversification doesn't just protect you from losses—it also limits your gains. And for investors who want to build serious wealth, that's the catch. Because most stocks actually underperform the market. Many produce long-term losses, and only a small handful are responsible for the majority of the market's long-term gains. The more you diversify, the more likely you are to own mediocre or poor companies.

Imagine you've found an exceptional company—with a strong business model, clear competitive advantage, and a leadership team that knows what it's doing. Why would you dilute this brilliant idea with 19 mediocre ones, just to "feel safer"? Every additional stock in your portfolio reduces the impact of your best idea.

A simple example illustrates this clearly: You invest $10,000 in one top-performing stock. That stock goes up 1,000%—your portfolio is now worth $110,000. Now imagine you split the same $10,000 across ten stocks. Your best stock still gains 1,000%, but now it only makes up 10% of your portfolio. The other nine are average—or worse. Result: your portfolio ends up at $20,000 or $30,000. Not bad—but far from what was possible.

In other words: even if you've hit the jackpot, your return is capped. Diversification, in this sense, is mostly one thing: insurance against ignorance—but it's a tax on conviction. It doesn't prevent losses—it just spreads them around. And it all but guarantees you'll never have a true financial breakthrough.

So why do so many investors do it anyway? The answer: because it feels safe. Because it's considered "responsible." Because it's easier to buy a little of everything than to recognize the best opportunity and commit fully. But great investments aren't about comfort—they're about clarity, conviction, and focus.

Diversification is not financial optimization—it's emotional reassurance. It helps you feel better during volatility, but it rarely makes you rich.

Of course, you can try to compensate with risk management— by cutting your losers early, for instance. That can work. But often, it's already too late: by the time you realize a position is failing, it's already caused significant damage. That damage then has to be made up by your winners. And this is where math begins to work against you—because losses aren't neutral; they're real.

Let's make this clear with a simple table:

Table 1: Required Gain to Recover a Loss

Loss (%)	Required Gain (%)
5 %	5.26 %
10 %	11.11 %
15 %	17.65 %
20 %	25.00 %
25 %	33.33 %
30 %	42.86 %
35 %	53.85 %
40 %	66.67 %
45 %	81.82 %
50 %	100.00 %
60 %	150.00 %
70 %	233.33 %
80 %	400.00 %
90 %	900.00 %

As you can see, realized losses pose a serious threat to your portfolio. If you lose 10% of your capital, you don't just need a 10% gain to get back to even—you need 11%. Why? Because after a loss, you're working with a smaller base. And the smaller that base becomes, the harder it has to work to recover. A 20% loss already requires a 25% gain to break even. A 50% loss needs a 100% recovery. And a 90% loss? Your remaining capital would need to increase almost tenfold—requiring a 900% gain!

Think about those numbers for a moment, and it becomes clear: losses grow *linearly*, but the gains needed to recover them rise *exponentially*. That's why repeatedly taking losses is so dangerous. And why it's critical to understand this dynamic before investing in a "broadly diversified" portfolio.

Let these numbers sink in, and you'll see that the "average model"—buying the index or "the market"—is, in truth, a very weak model. Because losses require exponentially higher gains to recover. Put differently: the Apples, Amazons, and Teslas of the world must perform extraordinarily well just to offset the losers. As you can see, the underlying math of this model doesn't work. It works *against* the investor.

If you invest in a broad portfolio with dozens of stocks—as is typically recommended—you're letting math work against you. New investors aren't told this. Instead, they're sold a sense of safety. But in my view, it's a false sense of safety.

If you're lucky and invest during a bull market—when stocks are mostly rising—this model can work reasonably well. But if your portfolio enters a sideways phase (think of the first decade of the 21st century), the weaknesses of this approach quickly become apparent. Whatever performs well in your portfolio is offset by the losing positions. You may have winners, but the losers prevent you from fully benefiting from them. At best, they keep your portfolio from collapsing completely. In reality, you've taken on a form of systemic risk that will drag on your performance over the long term.

One could argue that dividend strategies also hold losers. That's true—but with one crucial difference: even weak dividend stocks still pay income. A dividend investor can own a stock that's down 40%—and still realize a net gain because dividends continue to flow. In some cases, the dividends don't just offset the unrealized loss—they surpass it. In this case, the math works for the investor, not against them. That's why I recommend dividend strategies to those who want a steadier approach and a growing stream of supplemental income.

If we want the math to work for us—not against us—we must aim to keep as few losers in the portfolio as possible. One way to do this is to rigorously cut losing positions and hold only winners. This requires discipline, and in my experience, few investors are capable of it—even though it's entirely logical and sensible. Sooner or later, you'll have one or more winners in your portfolio, even if just by chance. If you can manage to remove the losers early—say, as soon as they hit a 10% loss—then the damage they can cause is limited, as Table 1 already made clear.

But then comes the second, more difficult question: when do you sell a winning stock? Even with a well-performing investment, you'll eventually have to decide whether to sit through a correction or sell and try to buy back later at a lower price.

As you can see, these are real-world questions that every investor must grapple with in order to manage a portfolio effectively. And experience shows that the stock you sell is often either never bought back, or you reenter too late—or too early. Most "active" investors wildly overestimate their timing ability. No one buys or sells at exactly the right time every time. That's why *holding* is often the better option when you have a winner.

There's a simple and often underrated model for holding long-term winners: after a stock doubles, take out your original investment and let the rest ride. How does this work? Let's say you invest $10,000 in Stock A. Once the stock doubles—gaining 100%—your position is worth $20,000. You sell half, reclaim your initial $10,000, and let the remaining $10,000 stay invested. What remains in your portfolio is now "risk-free"—you're playing with house money. Your capital is secured; the rest can run indefinitely—perhaps forever.

Let's take Apple as an example. If you had bought Apple shares in 2004 at a (split-adjusted) price of around $1, and sold half after a 100% gain one year later, you would have held the remainder through to today (March 2025). What would've happened? That remaining position would have returned about

10,900%. Your original $10,000 would have grown into over one million dollars—with an investment that carried no capital risk after 2005 because your principal was already taken off the table.

The idea sounds simple: wait for a double, take out your capital, never touch the rest. But here lies the challenge: discipline. Imagine, years later, seeing your remaining position grow to $300,000 or $500,000. Would you have the nerve to say, "I'm not selling—I'll let it run"? What seems easy on paper is much harder to stick with in real life—especially over time spans of 10, 15, or even 20 years. And that's the downside of this model. It demands patience. A lot of patience. And very few investors truly possess it.

Or do they? An aunt of mine has a stock portfolio. Every year, her bank sends her an account statement by mail. She gives it a quick glance and files it away. The folder goes back on the shelf—until next year. Not the worst approach, if you ask me...

Most Stock Market Fortunes Came from a Single Stock

All you need is one good idea per decade.

Warren Buffett

Most fortunes in the stock market were built on a single stock. That's a fact worth your reflection, dear reader. Because the common advice given to investors is to maintain a well-diversified portfolio. Let me be blunt: I don't know a single person who became wealthy that way. A diversified portfolio makes sense if you're already wealthy. And even then, it's debatable.

The real question every investor should ask is this: *Does this position have the potential to fundamentally change my financial future?* If the answer is no—then why take the position at all? Why put money into something that will have no real impact on your life?

Here's the truth: most of us are broke—at least compared to the lucky few who control millions or billions. And you will stay broke unless you're willing to do something exceptional. You'll stay right where you are: in the lower middle class, living paycheck to paycheck. This book isn't for those who have accepted that fate. It's written for the small, courageous group willing to take their financial future into their own hands.

Sure, I know investors who have earned decent returns over the past 15 years with a broadly diversified portfolio. But their gains weren't thanks to diversification—they came from two other factors. First, they were already wealthy. Second, the markets performed well between 2010 and 2025. Their wealth grew because they had a lot of capital to begin with—not because they "diversified wisely."

If you are not yet wealthy (and I consider anyone with under one million in assets *not* wealthy), then you need a different approach. You can't afford to invest the same way the wealthy do. Their primary goal is wealth *preservation*. That's already a serious achievement. But this book is about something else: how to become wealthy through the stock market—not how to preserve or grow wealth once it's already there.

Another crucial insight: hardly anyone gets rich by discovering some obscure penny stock and holding it for decades. Sure, those cases exist—but they're rare and mostly luck, like winning the lottery. Most successful investors owe their fortunes to well-known companies like Amazon, Apple, or Tesla—stocks everyone's heard of. You might think these investors got in early and simply held on for decades. That too is mostly a myth. Ask yourself: do you know anyone— aside from Jeff Bezos—who bought Amazon in 1998 and is still holding it today? Heroic stories sound great, but they're not necessary to succeed.

A perfect example: Warren Buffett. He didn't invest in Apple until 2016—quite late, considering the stock had already risen over 20,000% by then. And yet it became one of his best investments. Why? Because quality endures. What's good tends to stay good.

So no, you don't need secret knowledge or insider tips to invest successfully. In fact, the best opportunities are visible to everyone. What you do need is an excellent company—one that makes money. I would add: a company that makes *a lot* of money. And you need a clear plan for how to invest in it. That's what this book is about—developing a realistic, executable plan that can get you to your goal without having to hold for 30 years. Because let's be honest: most of us don't have the patience or the time to stick with something for 25 or 30 years. Of course, there are exceptions, and I'll present a few in this book—but they are just that: exceptions.

It can go faster—if you act with focus and discipline. The only requirement: you must understand *why* one great stock is all you need—not three, five, or ten. And you must be willing to stick to your plan.

Talk to people who've built a fortune in the stock market, and you'll hear the same story again and again: it was almost always one idea that made the difference. You'll rarely hear someone say, "I bought 50 quality stocks—carefully spread across industries, countries, and sectors—and never touched the portfolio for ten years. One morning I woke up, and I was rich." If a diversified portfolio led to significant wealth, it was usually because a lot of money was invested from the start.

But what about everyone else? What about those who don't have a fortune and enter the market with $10,000 or $20,000? The tragedy is that these beginner investors are given the same advice as the already wealthy: "Diversify. Spread your investments. Let the portfolio grow over time."

And what happens? With some luck, $10,000 becomes $20,000 or $30,000 over ten or twenty years. A nice result—but does that fundamentally change the investor's financial situation? Of course not. At best, they preserved their capital against inflation. At worst, they lost patience and ventured into risky trades. Many lose the little they had this way.

Clearly, what makes sense for the wealthy is useless for the rest. For someone starting with a small amount of capital, a broadly diversified portfolio is ineffective. Well, maybe if you had a 70-year investment horizon, you could benefit from the long-term effects of compounding. Then, someday, you might reach your first million. But who has that kind of patience? And who knows what a million will even be worth in 70 years?

Diversification is a fantasy for small investors. It's a comforting story that provides a sense of safety—but it doesn't move you forward financially. Whether you have $10,000 or $30,000, it won't make a meaningful difference in your life. You're not significantly "richer" or "wealthier."

And that's why generalized advice like this helps no one. Every financial situation is unique. The critical question must

21

be: *What do I expect from my stock market investment?* Do I want a safe, yet growth-oriented strategy? Do I want to invest regularly and build wealth slowly? Or do I want a real financial breakthrough—and do it decisively?

Depending on how you answer that question, dear reader, you'll need a different strategy—and a different investing philosophy. You might ask, "Why do I even need an investing philosophy?" The answer is simple: your philosophy keeps you on course—especially when things get tough. And they *will* get tough, I guarantee it. If you don't know why you're doing what you're doing, you'll likely give up—or join the long line of people who say they "tried investing once," but only ended up losing money.

Wealth Comes from Focus

There is a type of risk that receives little attention in the financial media: *opportunity risk*—the risk of *not* being invested when real opportunities arise. Many investors today regret not having bought at least one of the "Magnificent Seven" in time. And it almost wouldn't have mattered which one: Microsoft, Apple, Amazon, Meta, Nvidia—any of them would have been enough to build a fortune.

In my view, the right approach is to *focus*—not to diversify. The investor should find a single great idea and dedicate themselves fully to it. Wealth is built through concentration, not by spreading your attention thin. No one would open a bakery, a grocery store, and a hair salon at the same time—at least not successfully. Yet that's what many portfolios look like: a little bit of everything. But no professional works this way.

If you take only one thing from this book, let it be this: if you want higher returns, you shouldn't own *more*—you should own *less*, but with far greater conviction. That is the power of focus. And once you look at it mathematically, the advantage becomes undeniable.

Here's the key insight: concentration is not recklessness— it's clarity. Many investors see it as risky to concentrate their portfolio on just a few holdings. But that risk only exists if you don't know what you're doing. When you act with knowledge and conviction, concentration becomes a strategic asset.

Another benefit of focus is that you actually understand what you own. If you hold just a few stocks, you can dive deep into those businesses. You become an *owner*, not just a bystander. You follow the company's progress, earnings reports, and long-term outlook. This is manageable with five stocks—not with twenty or forty.

Now, the obvious question: isn't it dangerous to bet so heavily on just a few, or even a single, position?

The answer depends entirely on your approach. If you're guessing instead of researching, buying on impulse, or chasing hype, then yes—you're taking on serious risk. But if you carefully analyze a company, understand its business model, and trust its management and market position, then your decision is not risky—it's rational.

The real danger doesn't lie in how many stocks you hold, but in how little you know about them. That's why the formula for true wealth-building is not "as many as possible," but rather: *as few as necessary*—with full conviction.

The one-stock portfolio is for investors who are willing to concentrate on a single stock and hold it for years. It's not for everyone. But it's for those who find the right company—and have the mental strength to stick with it. In the end, concentration is not magic. It's math—plus courage.

You don't need 20 good ideas. One is enough. As with so many things in life, it's not the *many* that count—it's the *few* that truly matter. So direct your capital, your attention, and your patience to what *really* counts.

Find Something That Grows 20% Per Year

Albert Einstein is often quoted as saying, "He who understands compound interest earns it. He who doesn't, pays it." Whether the quote is genuinely his is uncertain—but its truth is beyond doubt. In the world of investing, there is hardly a force more powerful than compound interest. It outperforms intelligence, luck, and even great timing. Warren Buffett attributes the majority of his wealth to this very effect.

In the context of a one-stock portfolio, compound interest isn't just a useful idea—it *is* the entire strategy. If you find an outstanding company and hold it over time, you let its success work for you. The business grows, reinvests, and continually builds value. That's compound interest in action. When it works, it transforms modest beginnings into extraordinary results.

Many investors associate compound interest only with the reinvestment of dividends. That's certainly one valid path, and I'll share some examples of it in this book. But for a one-stock portfolio, dividend payouts aren't even necessary. Some of the most successful companies of recent decades—Amazon, Berkshire Hathaway, Alphabet, and Meta among them—have paid little or no dividends at all. Instead, they did something far more powerful: they reinvested their profits internally at exceptionally high returns on capital.

A company that doesn't pay a dividend retains its earnings and uses them to develop new products, expand into new markets, build infrastructure, enhance technology, or acquire other companies. Sometimes they even buy back their own shares, which boosts the value of the remaining shares. When management knows how to allocate capital effectively, the *intrinsic value* of the business increases—year after year. Even if no money ever lands in your bank account, your share in the business is quietly growing in value. Your stock becomes more valuable by nature of what the company is doing behind the scenes.

One of the most striking examples of this is *Amazon*. The company invested billions in expanding AWS, building logistics centers, and developing the Prime ecosystem. Every dollar reinvested laid the foundation for exponentially larger future profits. That's compound interest in its purest form. Despite never paying a dividend, Amazon's stock price mirrored the company's growing value in spectacular fashion. Just look at the numbers from 2001 to 2020. At the depths of the dot-com crash, Amazon traded for about $10 per share. By 2010, it was around $130. Just nine years later, it had risen more than twelvefold. By 2020, Amazon traded above $3,000—a 300x return since 2001. Amazon didn't pay out cash. It *worked for the investor* and expanded their ownership value internally.

Of course, there are good reasons for dividends. If you're seeking steady income, dividends can be useful. They allow you to draw cash or reinvest on your own terms. But if a company can reinvest its profits better than you could yourself, then your stake grows automatically—and often in a more tax-efficient way. Especially for long-term investors, this effect is incredibly valuable.

So, no—you don't need dividends to harness the power of compounding. What you need is a business that earns more than it spends, uses its surplus wisely, and grows consistently over time. When that happens, the intrinsic value per share rises steadily—and as a shareholder, you benefit indirectly, but substantially. Rather than asking whether a company is paying you, as a one-stock investor you should be asking: *Is this company multiplying year after year?*

To better grasp the power of this growth multiplier, let's look at some numbers. Imagine you invest $10,000 in a single stock. Depending on the annual rate of return, here's how that investment grows over time:

- At 10% per year, your capital grows to $25,937 after 10 years, $67,275 after 20 years, and $174,494 after 30 years.

- At 15% per year, you reach $40,455 after 10 years, $163,665 after 20 years, and $662,117 after 30 years.

- At 20% annual growth, your $10,000 becomes $61,917 in 10 years, $383,376 in 20 years, and a staggering $2,373,763 in 30 years.

This is the quiet power of exponential growth. It doesn't reveal itself immediately—but it is relentless, as long as you let it work. That's why compound interest is the most powerful force available to patient investors. It doesn't require a large starting amount. Just time, focus, and the right company. One glance at the numbers reveals a key truth: the longer you stay invested, the more powerful the compounding effect becomes. The biggest gains don't come in the early years—they come at the end. That's why compounding doesn't reward brilliance or timing—it rewards patience.

For a company to become a true compounding machine, three elements must come together. First, it needs consistent revenue growth—because more revenue means more potential earnings and, in turn, more value for shareholders. Second, it must maintain or expand its margins. The higher the margin, the more of each dollar ends up on the income statement—cash that can be reinvested. Third, the company must reinvest those profits internally at high returns.

The best businesses don't just sit on their earnings. They put them to work—developing new products, expanding into new markets, innovating in ways that generate new profits. This creates a kind of *flywheel effect*. Each cycle builds more momentum, accelerates the next one, and lifts the entire business to a higher level. The company multiplies—and so does your investment.

Let's look at how this works in practice. Apple is a textbook example. If you had invested $10,000 in Apple stock in 2007, that investment would be worth over $2.5 million by 2023. That outcome wasn't luck. Apple spent years expanding its ecosystem, building recurring revenue streams, developing its own chips, and investing heavily in innovation. At the same time, it bought back stock, further boosting earnings per share. Every move reinforced the next.

As an investor, your most important task is *not to interrupt this process*. For compound interest to work, you need a company capable of growing profitably. You must hold it long enough for the math to work in your favor. And you must not get shaken out by short-term losses, headlines, or popular opinion. The biggest threat to compounding isn't volatility—it's *you*.

What happens if you sell too early? Imagine buying Amazon in 2005 and holding it for just three years. The stock doubles, and you happily sell for a 100% gain. Sounds like a win. But if you had simply held on, your investment would have grown over the next 15 years by more than 100x. The difference is staggering. Selling early turns exponential potential into linear results—and that can cost you a fortune.

In investing, there are two kinds of growth. One is linear—steady, predictable, easy to grasp. The other is *exponential*. It starts off slow and unremarkable… then suddenly, it takes off. And here's the catch: most investors *think linearly*. But real wealth is created *exponentially*. Once you internalize that, you'll see what really matters. You don't need ten stocks. You don't need complex trading strategies. You don't need perfect timing. You need one exceptional stock—and patience.

Exponential growth means you're not just earning returns on your original capital—you're earning on your gains, and then on the gains of those gains. A simple example makes this clear: if you invest $10,000 in a stock earning 20% annually, you'll make $2,000 in the first year. In the second year, your gain is $2,400, because your base is now $12,000. In the third year, it's $2,880—and so on. Your return is compounding on a growing base each year. This is what makes exponential growth so powerful.

Let's stick with that example. You invest $10,000 once into a single stock that grows at an average of 20% per year. After 20 years, your investment has grown to about $383,000. After 30 years, it's worth more than $2.37 million. From a single purchase—no further contributions, no rebalancing. Just patience, and the power of math. This isn't fantasy. It's a natural law—and it can work for you.

The question is: why don't more people take advantage of it? The answer lies in human nature. We want to be rewarded quickly for our efforts. But exponential growth doesn't work that way. It feels slow at first. In the first five years, it looks like almost nothing is happening. After ten years, the results look solid, but not spectacular. But around year fifteen, the real magic begins—when growth starts to accelerate. Between year twenty and thirty, the miracle unfolds: this is when most of the wealth is created.

Once you understand this dynamic, your investment strategy changes. The math behind it is simple:

Future Value = Starting Capital × (1 + Return)^n

Where "Return" is your annual growth rate (e.g., 0.20 for 20%), and "n" is the number of years.

An example:

$10,000 × (1.20)^{30} = $2,373,763

That's not an optimistic guess—it's a formula. Your wealth doesn't grow through constant action, but through time. Many investors jump from stock to stock, chase quick profits, react to news, or sell in fear. But real wealth doesn't come from constant movement. It comes from patience, trust in a great company—and the quiet force of mathematics.

Why Not Holding Two or Three Stocks?

Many investors believe they're reducing risk by spreading their capital across multiple stocks. But this book takes a different approach. It's not just about concentration—it's about *radical focus*. Why should you own only *one* stock? Because maximum clarity and conviction lead to maximum results.

If you hold two stocks, it automatically means you're not fully convinced about at least one of them. Maybe you trust it 90%, or just 80%. But why would you invest your money in a company you don't *fully* believe in? Your best idea *is* your best idea. So why dilute it with weaker ones?

Even the math is against diversification. Imagine one of your stocks becomes an extraordinary winner. If your capital is split between two or three positions, the positive impact of that one outstanding stock on your overall portfolio is diminished. Instead of lifting your net worth dramatically, the gain is muted—simply because you didn't go all in.

If you find a company that's redefining innovation, disrupting an entire sector, and growing revenue and profits quarter after quarter—then it's not caution that's needed, but *conviction*. That's the moment to act—not to hedge.

The often-repeated claim that diversification reduces risk is, frankly, an illusion. The real risk doesn't lie in price fluctuations or short-term losses. The real risk lies in allocating capital to mediocre businesses that stagnate and fail to grow. Even worse is missing out on a truly great company because you've spread your money across a basket of average ones.

Failing to invest in a transformative business—or not holding it long enough—is the biggest risk of all: the lost opportunity to build real wealth. More stocks won't help you if none of them are truly strong. Two average companies won't get you ahead financially. What you need is one business you deeply believe is changing the world. If you don't feel that way about a stock, you shouldn't own it.

In reality, only one thing matters: *Do you own a winner or not?* History shows this time and again. Nearly every great fortune made in the stock market was built on a single company. So why should your approach be different?

The most important reason to focus on just one stock, in my view, is *mental clarity*. You only need to understand one company. Follow one management team. Monitor one industry. You don't have to worry about correlations, weightings, or rebalancing. And when you have extra capital, you know exactly where to put it. It hardly matters whether you add today, next week, or next month—especially if you're investing for the long term.

With only one stock, your strategy is clear and your attention undivided. The moment you add a second position, your focus starts to fragment. But if you want to become wealthy, focus is exactly what you need. If you've done your homework and truly believe you've found the right company, then your only task is this: *let the company do the work for you.*

You don't need ten ideas. You need one—and the discipline to stick with it. The hardest part is usually not *finding* the right company. In many cases, you already know it. Maybe you've been following it for years. Maybe you've watched it rise year after year—yet never bought in. The real challenge isn't finding. It's *holding*. It's staying in the position when others are selling. It's staying calm when the world around you goes crazy. It's having the discipline to ignore fear and follow your plan. And that's why you only need one stock. But for that one, you need absolute conviction that the company is changing the world.

Why Warren Buffett Is Also a One-Stock Investor

Warren Buffett is frequently presented in finance books, seminars, and articles as the ultimate example of cautious, long-term investing. In the public imagination, he stands for conservative strategies and broad diversification. But this perception is misleading. In reality, Buffett has never been a fan of diversification—he has always believed in *concentration*, and he has acted on that belief with full conviction.

His style was never about holding dozens of equally weighted positions. It was always about going big on the best ideas—and giving them time to flourish. Buffett once put it very clearly: *"Diversification is protection against ignorance. It makes little sense if you know what you are doing."*

Buffett doesn't chase trends or hot sectors. He looks for businesses with stable models, reliable cash flow, and competent management—at a reasonable price. And when he finds one, he doesn't hesitate. He invests decisively. A look at Berkshire Hathaway's stock portfolio in 2024 shows how consistently he has stuck to this approach:

- Apple makes up almost half the entire portfolio
- Bank of America around 9%

- American Express about 8%

- Coca-Cola 7%

- Chevron 6%

Roughly 80% of the portfolio's value is concentrated in just five companies. Apple alone accounts for 47%. That's not traditional diversification—that's focus. And it's focus built on deep trust in the underlying businesses.

Why does Buffett invest so heavily in a few positions? Because he understands that compound interest works best when you don't dilute your winners. If you're confident a company will outperform over the long term, it doesn't make sense to allocate only 5% or 10% of your capital to it. In that case, you're not reducing risk—you're reducing *opportunity*.

Buffett is clear about this. He's said that an investor's results depend largely on just a small handful of decisions. That's why he concentrates on those few critical bets—and lets them play out over years or even decades.

Another key to his success is his long-term perspective. Buffett doesn't trust "the market"—he trusts the *businesses* he owns. He doesn't panic when prices fall. He doesn't care about stock news or analyst forecasts. He focuses on the *intrinsic value* of the business—its cash flow, competitive advantages, and the quality of its leadership. And because he trusts in those fundamentals, he's able to hold large positions even when the broader market gets shaky.

His patience isn't theoretical—it's real. He has held Coca-Cola since 1988. American Express has been in the Berkshire portfolio since the early 1990s. And Apple—despite the late entry in 2016—has become the single most profitable investment of his career. So no, Warren Buffett is not the classic "diversifier" many people think he is. He is a focused investor. Someone who knows what he's doing—and has been successful with that approach for decades.

Why Passive Investing with ETFs Limits Your Returns

Passive investing with ETFs is widely seen as the safest, simplest, and most sensible way to build long-term wealth. And in many ways, that reputation is deserved. It's low-cost, requires no active stock selection, and has outperformed many actively managed funds over time. That alone is an impressive achievement. It's also the story that's been sold to millions of investors—and millions have bought it.

But this is precisely where the problem lies. Passive investing works—but it works so well at delivering average results that it becomes nearly impossible to get truly rich following that strategy.

So what does passive investing really mean? It means buying a basket of stocks that mirrors the overall market—like the S&P 500 or MSCI World—without making any individual decisions. You simply buy all the included companies in proportion to their market capitalization. This gives you broad diversification, moderate volatility—and a strictly average return. And that's the catch: this strategy is not designed to beat the market. It *is* the market.

Let's be clear: passive investing is not a bad strategy. It's far better than chasing penny stocks, following tips from online forums, or frantically trading based on headlines. But from a philosophical standpoint, it's built to deliver solid but mediocre outcomes. Historically, the S&P 500 has returned about 8 to 10 percent per year. That's fine. But at 8%, it takes nine years to double your money. A single stock growing at 25% annually can *10x* your capital in the same time. The math of compounding rewards boldness and focus. Choosing ETFs is choosing safety—but also accepting limitation.

So why is this strategy so popular? Simple: it provides a sense of security and control. You don't have to make any hard choices. You can't be wrong. But that also means you'll never be extraordinarily right. Index funds protect you from big mistakes—but also from big success. You won't fail, but you'll also never own a stock that grows tenfold or fiftyfold. You'll never beat the market, never build real, transformational wealth. Passive investing is the financial equivalent of a Volvo: safe, reliable—and entirely unremarkable.

The bigger problem runs deeper: when you buy an index, you don't just get winners like Apple or Nvidia—you also get the losers. You're buying struggling retailers, stagnant conglomerates, overleveraged banks, and outdated energy companies. Because index funds are weighted by market cap, many weak companies dilute the performance of the few strong ones. And that's what drags your total return down.

Here's a simple comparison to illustrate the point: If you had invested $10,000 in the S&P 500 in January 2009, you'd have about $40,000 today. If you had invested the same amount in Apple, you'd have over *one million dollars*.

Warren Buffett has always recommended ETFs only to those who don't know how to invest—or who are satisfied with average results. But if you want to break out financially, you need to understand this: passive investing won't lead to freedom. It's the waiting room, not the fast lane. The one-stock portfolio is not for the average investor. It's for people who understand compound interest and are willing to concentrate fully on a great business. For investors with the discipline to hold a single stock for many years—regardless of noise, corrections, or opinions. If you want your capital to grow exponentially, if you're aiming for real, asymmetric success, you won't find it in an index.

How to Belong to the "Strong Hands"

If you really want to make money in the stock market, you need to accept one simple idea: You are not a conventional investor. You are a speculator. And that's not an insult—quite the opposite. It means you're willing to take a real risk. You're doing exactly what everyone warns you not to do. You're putting all your chips on a single bet. To build wealth, you must concentrate your resources—your capital, your time, your energy—on one thing. Not two. Not five. One.

And that's exactly where the difference begins—between an investor, a trader, and a speculator. This distinction comes from the Hungarian stock market expert André Kostolany. The speculator, he said, has *thoughts*. Whether they are right or wrong doesn't matter at first. He has an *opinion*. But not on everything—only on one specific thing.

A speculator, for example, believes that *Tesla* is the best stock in the world. You might disagree—and that's fine. What matters is that the speculator has conviction. For him, nothing looks better than this one stock. Even if Tesla—like in March 2025—has fallen more than 50%, he doesn't doubt. On the contrary, he sees weakness as an opportunity to buy more.

That's conviction. That's posture. And that's exactly why this speculator is part of what we call the *"strong hands."* He buys when the crowd is selling. On the other hand, someone who holds Tesla as just one of five positions in a portfolio will likely sell—because he lacks conviction.

And this leads us to the core problem with diversification. Even if you hold just five stocks, you can't maintain the same level of clarity, focus, and commitment as someone who is all in on one idea. You can't love five people and claim to love them all the same. It's more powerful—in love as in investing—to choose one.

That's why you should pick one idea. One stock. One market. And stick with it. If the idea works out, the potential gains are massive. If it doesn't, you'll still gain something invaluable: experience. Because you didn't bet on "everything and nothing." You made a conscious decision. And that's the difference between playing around and having a strategy.

You will face setbacks. You will fail at times. But that's no reason to quit. It's the tuition fee everyone pays—in every field, in every profession. And if you truly understand that one good idea is all it takes to become financially free, then the journey is worth it.

Investing in a single stock is not for the hesitant. It goes against everything you'll read in mainstream financial advice or hear on the news. That's why the biggest challenge is *mental*. The buying part is easy. A few clicks—and it's done. But what comes afterward is much harder. You have to deal with *yourself*: your fear, your impatience, your doubt. You have to endure when others bail out. You have to believe when others lose faith. You have to belong to the *strong hands*.

Why Patience Is the Key to Stock Market Success

If you want the stock you've chosen to truly unfold its potential, you need one thing above all: *patience*. And having patience alone already sets you apart from the vast majority of investors. Patience is one of the rarest virtues in investing.

Let's assume you've chosen a growth-oriented company operating in a dynamic industry. These developments take time. A stock typically doesn't go from ten to a hundred—or even five hundred—within a week or a month. It usually takes years for its full potential to show. Whether that takes five, ten, or twenty years depends on the company. Anyone who embarks on this path must accept that they'll be invested for the long haul.

That's why it doesn't matter much whether you buy at nine, seven and a half, or eleven dollars. What matters is that you start. That first purchase gives you a feel for the stock. Pullbacks are not a threat—they're an invitation. They offer the opportunity to add to your position at better prices. It might take months or even years to build your full position. And even if you've been invested for five or ten years already, there's nothing wrong with continuing to buy whenever the opportunity presents itself. Significant positions don't happen overnight. They're built gradually, with growing conviction.

Of course, it's theoretically possible to become a millionaire from a single $1,000 investment—just like the Amazon example. But let's be honest: aside from Jeff Bezos, hardly anyone pulled that off. Almost no one buys right at the bottom and then holds for decades. And the good news is—you don't have to. Take a look at Amazon's long-term stock performance. Over the last 25 years, there have been plenty of entry points.

Figure 1: Amazon, Quarterly Chart, 1997–2025

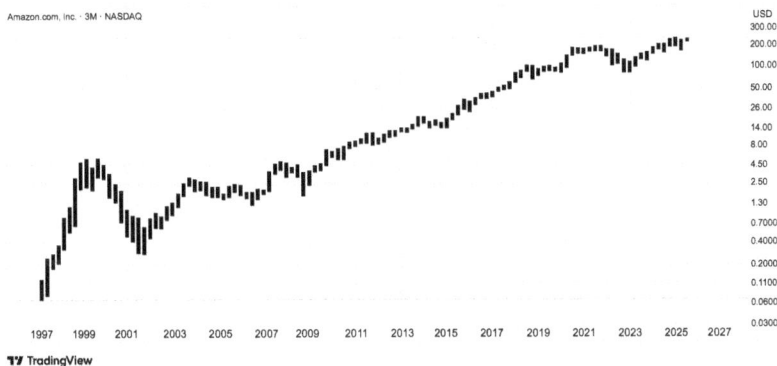

Amazon.com, Inc. · 3M · NASDAQ

USD
300.00
200.00
100.00
50.00
26.00
14.00
8.00
4.50
2.50
1.30
0.7000
0.4000
0.2000
0.1100
0.0600
0.0300

1997 1999 2001 2003 2005 2007 2009 2011 2013 2015 2017 2019 2021 2023 2025 2027

TradingView

As you can see, you could have bought the stock at virtually *any point* over those 25 years. As of April 2025, it's still buyable. There was hardly a phase when some analyst didn't claim the stock was too expensive or vastly overvalued.

But if you share the perspective of this book, you'll recognize such opinions as irrelevant. Growth stocks almost always look overpriced—until suddenly, they're not. The long-term chart makes one thing clear: timing is less important than conviction and patience. If you believe in the business model, you can enter almost anytime and still succeed.

That also means you should only invest in companies where you have good reason to believe in the long-term sustainability of their business model. With Amazon, this may not have been clear in the late 1990s or early 2000s. But by 2005 or 2006, it was obvious to anyone paying attention that Amazon was no longer a flash in the pan—it was here to stay. Anyone who bought around then would have multiplied their money by a factor of at least one hundred. Not even the financial crisis would have changed that (Amazon dropped more than 65% in 2008!).

If you're watching daily charts—or even shorter intervals like hourly charts—you're not suited for this perspective. The minimum time unit I recommend for the one-stock portfolio is the weekly chart—ideally, the monthly chart. Anything below that is just "market noise" and has nothing to do with a company's fundamentals.

Why should a long-term investor care if Amazon drops from 215 to 195 dollars when he bought his first shares at $12 or $16? These swings exist so that the "weak hands" sell in panic and the "strong hands" can buy at a discount. As Amazon's long-term chart shows, this happened dozens of times in the last 25 years. And each time, it was an opportunity to buy—and it still is.

Viewed this way, "getting rich from a single stock" is simple. So why do so few investors succeed? There are several reasons.

Chief among them is the required long-term perspective. You need patience and steadiness to buy during corrections. Most investors lack these traits. They're absent because society and media have conditioned us to think short term.

Like every growth process, there will be times when the young "plant" bursts with energy and the stock soars. But growth also involves consolidation. These consolidation phases can stretch out and involve deep drawdowns—sometimes more than 40%. The investor must sit through them.

You must adopt the mindset of a tree. In spring, the branches burst forth, and the sap flows to the outermost leaves. In summer, the tree stands in full glory, and it seems like it will always be that way. But every observer of nature knows what comes next: a long winter in which the tree "digests" what was achieved. Growth pulls back. The tree sleeps.

As an investor, you must understand your stock will go through the same phases. Of course, those only loosely connected to the company will claim the growth is over and it's time to sell. The investor should resist these voices—or better yet, ignore them completely. Because just as spring inevitably returns, there will be times when the stock soars again—and times when it bores you with inactivity. Worse yet, there will be times when previous gains are gradually wiped out—as if spring's growth had meant nothing.

You'll experience all of these emotions as an investor. The greatest challenge is staying calm during the withdrawal phases—and doing *nothing*.

The Power of Deep Conviction

If there's one thing I hope to achieve with this book, it's to help you, dear reader, see the stock market in a completely different light. For most people, the market appears as a vast universe full of opportunities. Goldmines seem to be hidden everywhere, and it's easy to be overwhelmed by the sheer abundance of choices.

But that's only one side of the coin. This universe of opportunities is useless if you don't have a compass. Because this world is also filled with noise, fear, and distraction. In such a world, conviction is your only compass.

The one-stock portfolio is not for the faint of heart. It's not about chasing trends, reacting to price moves, or trying to outsmart the market. It's about placing your chips on one exceptional company and letting it grow—for years, maybe even decades. That's only possible if you possess something most investors never truly develop: *real conviction.*

Conviction is not certainty. It's not arrogance. And it's not blind loyalty. Conviction is clarity plus courage. It means knowing exactly what you own, why you own it, and what would have to change for that no longer to be true. It's intellectual— based on thorough research, understanding, and logic. And it's emotional—rooted in trust in your own process and a high tolerance for discomfort.

Deep conviction doesn't come from the gut. It comes from rigorous analysis. Before investing in a single stock, you should understand the company's business model, competitive position, financial metrics, and growth outlook. This foundation doesn't just create confidence in your investment—it minimizes the risk of betting on a company that could ultimately fail.

Why does this matter? Because without conviction, you'll get shaken out long before the power of compounding can take effect. With conviction, you can weather storms that others won't survive.

That's why most investors can't hold a stock for ten years. They don't have conviction—they have *conditions*:

- "I'll hold as long as it keeps going up."
- "I'll stay in as long as it beats the market."
- "I'll sell if there's a crash."

Those aren't convictions. They're exit clauses.

That's why people sell in panic after a 30% drop—and then chase whatever's hot at the moment. That's why they underperform their own stocks. The market punishes shallow conviction. But it rewards deep conviction.

So how do you build real conviction in a stock? You don't just decide to be "convicted." Conviction is something you earn over time—by doing the hard work others avoid. Can you explain how the company makes money—and why that's sustainable? Do you understand its competitive edge? Do you trust management to allocate capital wisely? Is the company riding a trend that could last ten or twenty years? Would you want to own the entire company, if you could?

If the answer is yes, then you're not gambling—you're investing with clarity.

In a one-stock portfolio, you can't offset uncertainty by diversifying. Your entire advantage lies in your ability to stay the course through rough patches. That means believing in your thesis even when other stocks seem to be doing better. It means trusting in time, not timing. Conviction is not a feeling—it's a system. A decision you make once, and then reaffirm again and again.

Because in a one-stock portfolio, it's not the stock that makes you rich—it's your ability to hold it when no one else will. Deep conviction means investing in a stock as if it were your own business. And in a way, it *is*. When you own shares—especially a large position, as you would in a one-stock strategy—it starts to feel like you own the whole company. You become part of its unfolding story. You benefit from its success—but you also carry its challenges and setbacks. You grow with it until it finds its rightful place in the market.

That's a world apart from buying a stock just to flip it a few weeks later. That's the behavior of a tourist—someone who visits a foreign country for a week or two but never becomes a local.

A true investor goes deep. He takes the time to know the business intimately. With growing conviction, he builds a significant position that can make him wealthy—just as the founders of the company might become rich if their vision succeeds.

Such an investor isn't a tourist. He is someone who moves to a new country, owns a home, learns the language, and adopts the local customs. You can't easily shake that person. He is positioned to seize every opportunity the new land has to offer.

Don't Buy a Stock—Buy a Business

A one-stock portfolio is not just a financial decision—it's a philosophical one. Most market participants trade tickers, symbols, and momentum. They buy what's hot, follow chart patterns, chase upgrades, or panic on bad news. But if you're going to bet everything on a single asset, you can't think like a trader. You have to think like an *owner*.

The one-stock strategy means you're not just buying a piece of paper. You're taking a stake in a living, breathing business—one with people, customers, a strategy, and a future.

A stock is not a lottery ticket. When most investors say, "I like this stock," what they usually mean is, "The chart looks good," or "It went up last week," or worse, "Everyone's talking about it."

But price action isn't the same as business quality. Popularity doesn't mean durability. A stock is more than a chart—it's a claim on future profits. And that only matters if the business behind the stock is truly great. So what does it mean to think like an owner? If you owned 100% of the company, you'd ask:

Are we selling more than last year?

Are our customers loyal?

Do we have a competitive edge?

Can we keep growing for 10 or 20 years?

Is our management making sound, long-term decisions?

That's how the best investors think—Buffett, Munger, Lynch, and others.

If you think like an entrepreneur, you'll focus on products, margins, vision, return on capital, and durable advantages—not headlines or short-term earnings misses.

And by the way, the math is on the owner's side. What drives a stock over 10 or 20 years? Not market sentiment or hype. It's revenue growth, margin expansion, reinvested profits, buybacks, and returns on capital. Those are *business fundamentals*—not trading signals. If the business is exceptional, the stock price *must* eventually follow.

Take *Starbucks*, for example. In the short term, the stock might be volatile. But long-term, it's remarkably stable. The company sells an addictive product, with strong margins, global expansion potential, and a powerful brand. If you buy Starbucks, you're buying a business model—not just a logo.

Before you invest, ask yourself: How does this company make money?

Would I feel comfortable owning the entire business, if I could?

Owning a stock is like choosing a business partner. It's your passive employee—working 24/7 to grow your wealth. Would you pick a business partner based on a chart pattern? Or would you choose based on integrity, track record, ambition, and competitive strength?

The stock you choose isn't just a symbol—it represents a person, a product, and a plan. So get to know it better than anyone else. Don't just buy a stock. Buy a business you understand. Buy a machine that can generate value over decades. And then do what great entrepreneurs do: stay the course, think long-term, don't panic during setbacks, and let compounding do its work.

Because in a one-stock portfolio, your wealth depends on one thing only: the quality and resilience of the company behind the ticker. If the business is exceptional, your outcome will be too. Building a one-stock portfolio is not like building a traditional investment portfolio. It's not about reducing volatility or following the market. It's about going *all in* on one great company—just like a founder goes all in on their startup.

In fact, investing in a single stock is much more like *founding* a company than it is like conventional investing. That's why most people can't do it—because it requires the same qualities that successful entrepreneurs need.

Does that mean you have to be an entrepreneur to succeed with this strategy?

Not at all. But the commitment and discipline to follow through with it are very similar. The long-term mindset is the same. The setbacks—market corrections—are inevitable. Anyone who's ever built a business will tell you that. (So will the author of this book, who's built several.)

Practically speaking, buying a stock is far easier than building a company. But the psychological challenges come close. Entrepreneurs don't run 50 businesses at once. They focus on *one*. They invest capital, time, research, energy, and belief into a single mission—not two or ten. Why? Because they believe in the idea. They see long-term value. They want to build something scalable. Owning a single stock is a mindset. It says: "I believe in this company so much, I'm willing to build my future on it." That's exactly what a founder does.

Of course, there are differences between the work of an entrepreneur and the task of a focused investor. A founder builds a company from scratch, while an investor acquires shares in a business that's already successful. The founder risks both capital and time; the investor risks capital—time is his multiplier. The entrepreneur develops a product for which there is a market, assembles a team, and shapes a company culture defined by leadership and vision. The investor, on the other hand, seeks profit and value creation. The founder focuses on an idea, the investor on the performance of that idea.

Essentially, as an investor, you're partnering with the founder and joining him on his business journey—because you own a piece of the company. If you've ever seen how a private equity firm invests in a startup, you'll know what I mean. These people inspect every brick and every nail to make sure nothing is rotten underneath. And beyond that, founders are often required to present detailed monthly reports to their investors. That's exactly the level of involvement you should feel when choosing your company. After all, you're the one entrusting your capital to these people.

Before founding a company, entrepreneurs draft a business plan. That's why you, before committing your capital to a single stock, should do the same—whether on paper or in your mind. You need clear answers to key questions like:

- What does this company do that no one else can?
- How large is its potential market?
- Is the customer base loyal—and growing?
- Can the company defend its position long term?
- Is the leadership world-class?
- How can this business earn more five to ten years from now than it does today?

This isn't just about investing. It's about aligning yourself strategically with one business you understand deeply. When a company hits a rough quarter, founders don't just sell their stake. They adapt, reassess, and keep building. As a long-term, concentrated investor, you act the same way. You don't panic at corrections, react to headlines, or think in days—you think in *decades*.

Market volatility and fluctuations in your stock aren't threats. They reflect seasonal cash flow, market sentiment, or the investment cycle of the business. Just like a business owner, you don't abandon ship when the wind shifts. You steer, adjust, and continue the voyage.

A founder doesn't say, "Let me spread my energy across 10 startups, just in case this one doesn't work." They focus. They concentrate—because they know extraordinary returns only come from deep commitment. That's exactly how the one-stock portfolio works. You need deep research, long holding periods, and an unwavering belief in the growth story. And yes, you'll also need—like any entrepreneur—emotional resilience.

Consider Ray Kroc, the man behind *McDonald's*. He didn't build 10 fast food chains—he built one, better than anyone else. Warren Buffett, too, thinks like a business owner. When he buys a company, he often holds it for life—because he's not buying a stock, he's buying the business.

You are not a fund manager. You're a focused investor with the courage to concentrate—like a founder. When you invest in a single stock, you're not making a passive bet. You're making a strategic decision to partner with excellence. You're saying:

"I know this business."

"I believe in its vision."

"I trust the math of compounding."

"And I'm willing to ride through storms—because the foundation is sound."

That's not random. That's entrepreneurship—with a stock ticker. So stop thinking like someone buying a piece of paper. Start thinking like someone building a financial future—one great business at a time.

Why We Underestimate Trends That Can Last for Decades

In a world obsessed with novelty, most investors suffer from a dangerous affliction: they get bored with what works. They ignore the obvious, chase the complicated, and underestimate the trends that quietly, steadily, and relentlessly reshape the world—sometimes over decades. Within the context of a one-stock portfolio, this mistake can be fatal. If you are betting your financial future on a single idea, it must be big, durable, and—ideally—underestimated. That's exactly what long-term trends often are.

In this chapter, we'll explore the following questions: Why do investors repeatedly overlook the power of slow but transformational trends? Why is early and patient better than smart and busy? And how can you use simple, enduring trends to build extraordinary wealth with a single stock?

Most investors believe: "If it's simple, it can't be powerful." So they chase the next AI play or the hottest biotech IPO. Meanwhile, right before their eyes, a few clear forces are quietly transforming the world:

- Cloud computing
- E-commerce

- Electric vehicles

- Demographic shifts

- The digitization of money (e.g., Bitcoin)

And yet, few investors fully capitalize on these forces. The obvious doesn't seem exciting. But here's the truth: the greatest fortunes aren't built through complexity—they're built through clarity. There are five psychological traps that cause investors to underestimate or ignore long-term trends:

1. **Short attention span**

   We live in a world of notifications and dopamine hits. Following a single idea for 10 years feels like laziness— not strategy. But boredom isn't a signal to sell. It's a signal that you're doing everything right.

2. **Recency bias**

   If a trend hasn't worked for the last 6 to 12 months, we assume it's "over." But short-term market movements don't reflect long-term adoption. Amazon, for example, went nowhere from 2000 to 2008—then increased 100-fold.

3. **Need for novelty**

   We confuse change with opportunity. We think the next trend must be better. But often, the "old" trend is still in its infancy. In 2012, people said online shopping was "done." By 2020, the pandemic showed e-commerce had only just begun.

4. **Underestimating exponential growth**

   We think in straight lines. But trends compound. A market that grows 20% per year for 10 years doesn't rise 200%—it grows 519%. What looks "slow" today can become unimaginably large tomorrow.

5. **Media noise**

   The news cycle focuses on what's new—not on what's working. As a result, investors get distracted, discouraged, or derailed—and miss the big moves.

Let's look at real-world examples of "obvious" trends that could have made you wealthy. Some of them have been compounding quietly for decades.

1. Currency Devaluation and Distrust in Fiat Money

Figure 2: Gold 3-Month Chart, 2000–2025

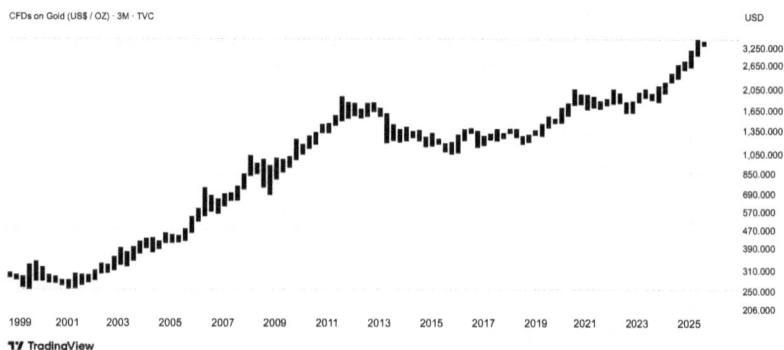

In the year 2000, gold traded below $300 per ounce. By 2011, it had reached over $1,900—a sixfold increase in a decade, outperforming most equity markets. Why? Because of low real interest rates, growing global debt, central bank expansion, and the devaluation of the U.S. dollar.

Since then, gold has reached new all-time highs in 2024–2025, driven by a long-term erosion of trust in fiat currencies. This is a slow-moving global macro trend—not flashy, but extremely powerful.

2. Supercycles in Oil and Energy

Figure 3: Oil Price (WTI), Monthly Chart 1999–2008

Light Crude Oil Futures · 1M · NYMEX

TradingView

Trend: Underinvestment in supply + sustained demand. Periods of underinvestment in oil production (such as 2015–2020) often lead to supply shocks and price spikes.

Examples:

- Oil prices rose from $10/barrel in 1999 to over $140 in 2008

- Energy stocks (e.g., Exxon, Chevron) outperformed in massive cyclical waves

- LNG (liquefied natural gas) has become a global growth industry due to rising energy security concerns

Companies like Canadian Natural Resources (CNQ) and ConocoPhillips have quietly delivered strong returns, thanks to global demand and capital discipline. Commodities may be cyclical—but supercycles are driven by deep trends.

3. Costco (COST)

Figure 4: Costco, 3-Month Chart 1986–2025

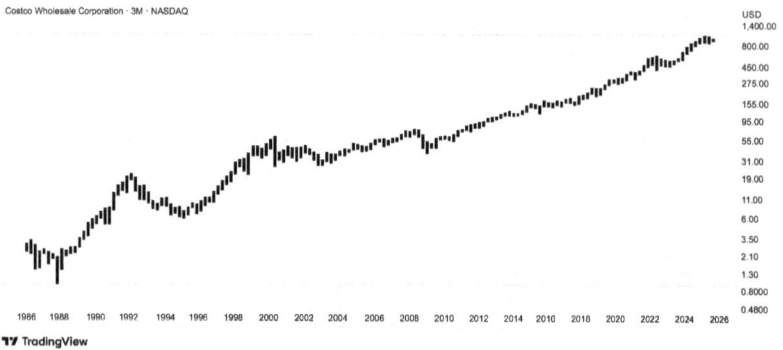

Trend: Value for consumers, loyalty, and subscription retail. Costco may seem "boring," but it has benefited for over 30 years from the following structural tailwinds:

- Everyday low prices
- High customer retention
- Steady global expansion
- House brand dominance (e.g., Kirkland Signature)

The result? From 2013–2023, the stock grew at 18% per year—outperforming many tech growth stocks, and with less volatility. Why? Because Costco stayed consistent. And the trend isn't over.

4. Monster Beverage (MNST)

Figure 5: MNST, 3-Month Chart 2003–2025

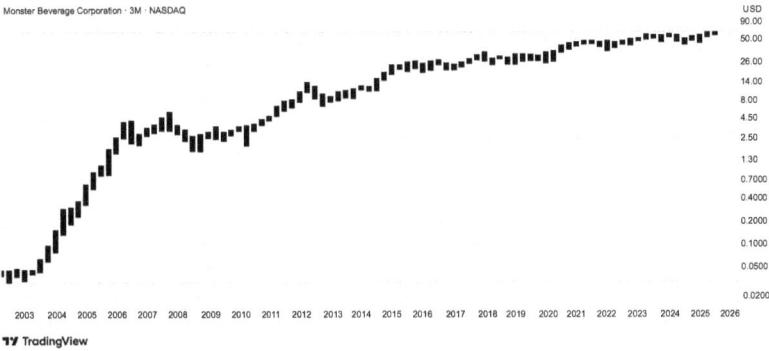

Trend: Health-conscious caffeine meets global branding. Monster capitalized on the energy drink wave. MNST is one of the best-performing U.S. stocks of all time—compounding over 30% annually for more than two decades.

Market cap rose from $200 million to over $60 billion. It wasn't a tech stock or a hype play—just a niche consumer trend paired with unwavering consistency.

5. L'Oréal (OR, Paris)

Figure 6: OR, 3-Month Chart 1987–2025

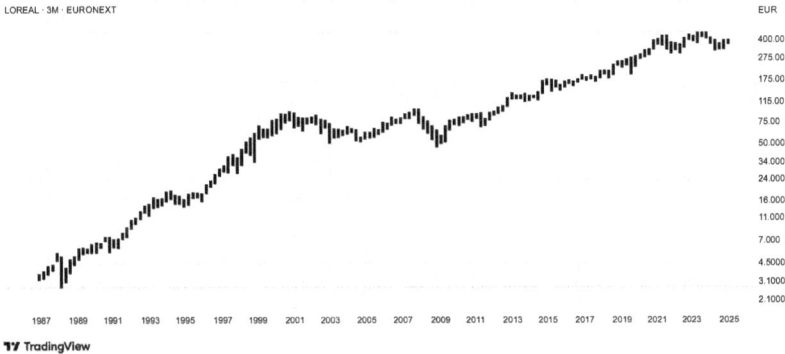

Trend: Global beauty, luxury, and the desire to consume. The French cosmetics giant L'Oréal has ridden the long wave of growing demand for affordable luxury. The result? A nearly 20-fold increase in its stock price over two decades—plus steady dividend growth. The company has quietly built massive wealth by serving a global, cross-generational trend.

6. Agriculture – Deere & Company (DE)

Figure 7: DE, 3-Month Chart 1968–2025

Deere & Company · 3M · NYSE

Trend: Global food demand and mechanized agriculture. John Deere has benefited from a growing global population, the modernization of farming, and the rise of smart agriculture. Though cyclical, the company has evolved into a quiet industrial-tech powerhouse with a real competitive moat.

7. Bitcoin and the Monetization of Scarcity

Figure 8: BTC, Monthly Chart 2012–2025

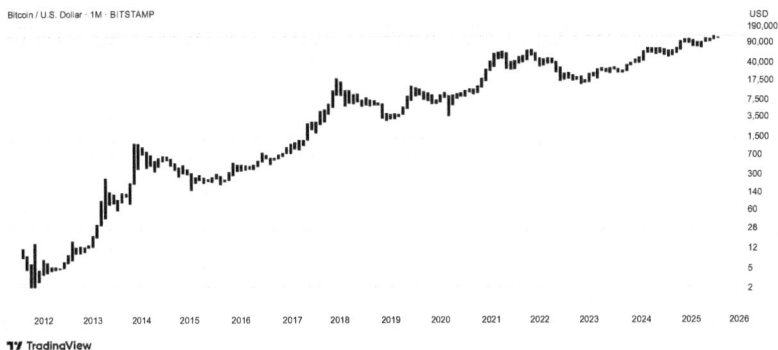

Bitcoin / U.S. Dollar · 1M · BITSTAMP

USD
190,000
90,000
40,000
17,500
7,500
3,500
1,500
700
300
140
60
28
12
5
2

2012   2013   2014   2015   2016   2017   2018   2019   2020   2021   2022   2023   2024   2025   2026

TradingView

Trend: Digital money with fixed supply. Is Bitcoin too obvious? Then why do so few investors hold it for more than 2–3 years? Most either never got in—or no longer dare to—because Bitcoin seems "too volatile," "too simple," or "already too high."

All these trends are either slow and obvious—like gold, Costco, or oil—or global and structural, like L'Oréal, Deere, or Monster Beverage. They act as long-term engines of compounding growth. These companies benefit from recurring revenues, pricing power, and demand bottlenecks—and are often underestimated by Wall Street. They don't make headlines. They make returns.

Not every trend is loud. Some just quietly keep winning. Most investors chase the next big thing. The contrarian path? Find a seemingly "boring" trend with 10–20 years of potential left—and stick with it. You don't need something new. You need something durable.

So when evaluating a candidate for your one-stock portfolio, ask yourself:

- Is this trend demographic, structural, or scarcity-driven?
- Does this company serve a need that's growing in strength?
- Am I willing to hold it through boredom, noise, and cycles?

Big money isn't made by identifying complexity. It's made by holding on to simplicity—longer than everyone else.

How do you recognize a fundamental trend with staying power? Ask yourself:

Is global adoption still in the early stages?

Can this trend open new doors for the company—via products, services, or ecosystems?

Are smart capital allocators backing it for the long haul?

Are people saying: "It's too late"? (That's usually the middle, not the end.)

A great trend lasts 10 to 30 years. But most investors only jump in during the first 18 months. In a one-stock portfolio, the long-term trend *is* your core thesis. You're not betting on price action—you're aligning yourself with an unstoppable force: decentralized finance (Bitcoin), data and AI (Nvidia), digital consumption (Apple, Meta), or platform economics (Amazon, Shopify).

The obvious is often underrated. The irony of the stock market is that everyone's searching for secrets—while wealth often comes from doing simple things *very* well, for *a very long time.*

Don't dismiss a trend because it's obvious. Don't give up because it's boring. Don't underestimate it because it doesn't spike. Investing isn't about excitement. It's about picking trends that outlast the hype. The best trends hide in plain sight. The smart investor picks one—and holds on.

The Hardest Part of a One-Stock Portfolio: Doing Nothing

The greatest challenge for any one-stock portfolio investor is learning to do... *absolutely nothing.* The job of a long-term investor is, more than anything else, to "watch the grass grow" or "watch the paint dry." And that's exactly where most people fail. Doing nothing—waiting, observing, being patient—is a rare trait in the modern world. But it's precisely this trait that builds real wealth.

Unlike the entrepreneur who is constantly acting, the long-term investor must learn to sit still—especially when their stock is correcting or going sideways for months. The investor must resist the urge to interfere and summon the patience to let the company they believe in unfold in its own time.

At the core of investing lies a paradox: the more you trade, tinker, and optimize, the worse your results usually are. This is especially true in a one-stock portfolio. You've done your research. You've chosen your company. You believe in it. Now comes the hardest part: do nothing. That means: don't check prices several times a day. Don't react to headlines. Don't try to outsmart the market. Just hold.

Doing nothing—watching grass grow—is incredibly difficult. We never learned how. In fact, most of life taught us the opposite: act now, show results, be efficient. Long-term thinking is rarely taught—neither by parents, nor in school, nor at universities. There's no class called "Doing Nothing 101."

I speak from experience: when you hold just one position, staying inactive is hardest. But it's the path to real wealth—and the point where most investors break.

Let's give the idea of doing nothing a deeper context. In Taoism, there is a principle called *Wu Wei* (无为). It doesn't mean laziness or apathy—it means "effortless action," or more accurately: "non-interference with the natural flow of things." Taoist sages observed that nature never forces, rushes, or struggles—and yet everything gets done. Rivers flow. Trees grow. Seasons change.

There is a powerful force in letting things unfold at their natural pace. A one-stock portfolio is *Wu Wei* applied to money: You choose an excellent company, you trust in the long-term power of compounding—and then you step aside and let the process work.

"Do nothing, and nothing will be left undone."

Laozi

Why is it so hard for us modern humans to do nothing? Simple: it feels wrong. Modern life urges us: act! Improve! Hustle! So when your stock drops 15% in a week, trades sideways for 12 months, or lags behind some trendy AI name, you'll likely feel anxious. You'll think: "Should I be doing something?"

But especially then, your job is not to act—it's to understand, observe, and endure. The real skill of an investor lies in not reacting.

What happens when you can't sit still? Most investors underperform their own investments. Studies show that the average investor earns 3–4% less per year than the mutual fund they invest in. Why? Overtrading, panic-selling, and trying to time the market. Even with incredible companies like Apple (multiple corrections of 40–60%), Amazon (a 90% drop during the dot-com crash), or Nvidia (many drawdowns over 50%), most investors made no money—because they didn't stay invested. The price of exponential wealth is patience in the face of chaos.

Zen Buddhism offers a useful lens here. It teaches that clarity arises from emptiness, not noise. A core practice is *zazen*— just sitting. No goal, no striving. Just presence. That's how the one-stock investor behaves: sitting quietly, anchored in conviction, without meddling in the process. Your edge is not in doing more. It's in inner stillness amid a noisy world. As a Zen proverb says:

"When nothing is done, nothing is left undone."

Here's another analogy I love: the growth of a plant. Everyone understands this. A plant is not a machine. You don't pull it to make it grow faster. You don't dig up its roots every week to check progress. You water it, give it light—and let it grow.

Wealth grows like life itself—it needs time and calm, not haste and meddling. Doing nothing is not passive. It's active restraint. It's discipline disguised as stillness.

So how do you practice doing nothing? Let me be honest: *good investing is boring*. But boredom isn't failure—it's a signal that you're doing it right. Stillness is a superpower. Charlie Munger once said: "The big money is not in the buying or selling, but in the waiting."

In Zen, this is called *No-Mind*—action without ego, response without panic, life without friction.

In a one-stock portfolio, stillness is not just a tactic. It's the entire game.

Find a great company. Buy it at a reasonable price (or use dollar cost averaging to build your position). And then…do nothing.

You can count on one thing: the world will panic. The media will scream. Other investors will flinch. But you'll be the still water. Let the river of time build your wealth in peace.

You don't plant a tree just to dig it up every month. You plant it once, nurture it early—and let it grow for years. The most radical act in modern investing is silence. The most powerful force is time. The most underestimated skill is *doing nothing*.

Part 2: How Do You Find the Right Stock?

Most Stocks Are Losers

Now that we've explored the mental foundation required for this unique strategy, we turn to the central question: How do you find the right stock for a one-stock portfolio?

Here's something that's rarely said out loud—despite being statistically undeniable: Most stocks underperform. Many go nowhere. A large number actually lose money. And the more stocks you buy, the higher the odds that your portfolio will include mediocre or poor companies. As a result, you automatically dilute the impact of your best idea.

Studies have shown that 80% to 90% of long-term market gains come from a small minority of stocks. One study by Hendrik Bessembinder (Arizona State University) found that just 4% of all publicly traded U.S. stocks were responsible for the entire net gain of the stock market over the last several decades. In other words, most stocks don't even beat the market. A few exceptional ones do—and they carry the rest along with them.

This is exactly why diversification doesn't make sense. When you spread your bets widely, you almost guarantee that you'll own more losers than winners. If you go to the effort of identifying a truly exceptional company, it becomes only logical to concentrate your capital in that one stock. Every additional stock you add increases the risk of introducing an underperformer. You dilute the effect of your best idea—both mathematically and psychologically.

The more stocks you own, the more average or even losing companies you're likely to hold. This is an uncomfortable truth that almost no one talks about. But once you understand the math—and have the courage to act on it—committing to a single stock becomes the most logical and potentially the most profitable decision of your investing life.

What Makes a Stock a Compounding Machine?

A "compounding machine" is a stock you buy once, hold for decades, and watch as a modest investment quietly transforms into life-changing wealth—not through hype or luck, but through repeatable growth. A compounding stock isn't flashy—it's consistent. It isn't exciting—it's inevitable. But how do you recognize the rare businesses that can quietly—and massively—build wealth over time? What exactly makes a stock one of those rare compounding machines? Let's take a closer look.

1. High Return on Invested Capital (ROIC)

How efficiently does the company turn its money into more money? A true compounding machine reinvests every dollar it earns at high returns—not just once, but repeatedly. This means each reinvested dollar generates even more profit. Growth funds itself. The business doesn't need constant outside capital or excessive debt. Look for a sustainable ROIC above 15%. A high return on equity (ROE) is also desirable, along with expanding operating margins over time.

Example: Apple invests billions in R&D and product design, leading to higher-margin devices, sticky software ecosystems, and lucrative services. These reinvestments steadily create value.

2. A Long Reinvestment Runway

It's not enough to have high returns—you also need a market where capital can be deployed for years to come. A compounding machine operates in a sector with a massive addressable market and room for sustained organic growth. You want a steady flow of customers or continuous product expansion. Ideally, competitors are weak, shrinking, or irrelevant to this winner.

Example: Amazon started with books, expanded into all retail categories, then into cloud computing (AWS), logistics, advertising—and beyond. That's a runway that can last for decades.

3. Strong Competitive Moats

The wider the moat, the longer the compounding runway. Without protection, high profits invite competition. A compounding machine needs a lasting advantage that gets stronger over time. We'll explore different types of moats in more detail in another chapter, but for now: moats protect margins, customer relationships, and market share—and they enable uninterrupted growth.

4. Predictable, Recurring Revenue

Compounding loves stability. The best businesses have either subscription models (Netflix, Microsoft), repeat purchase cycles, long-term customer loyalty (Apple), or high customer lifetime value (CLV). This predictability allows for better capital planning, consistent reinvestment, and fewer operational shocks.

Example: Microsoft's shift to subscription-based Office 365 and Azure made revenues more predictable and margins more resilient—fueling years of compounding growth.

5. Strong Free Cash Flow and Capital Discipline

A compounding machine must generate one thing: real cash, not just accounting profits. And that cash must be used wisely. Look for companies that consistently produce free cash flow and reinvest it efficiently (not just buying back stock at any price). The company should avoid unnecessary dilution or overpriced acquisitions, and it should be able to grow without excessive debt.

Example: Alphabet (Google) generates tens of billions in free cash each year, funding innovation and buybacks—without compromising its core compounding engine.

6. Visionary and Rational Management

Compounding requires discipline (not overpaying for growth), vision (understanding where the world is headed), and patience (resisting the pressure of short-term performance). You want leaders who think in decades, not quarters—who understand capital allocation and build a culture that attracts long-term talent and innovation.

A compounding machine might look unremarkable from the outside, but inside it's quietly brilliant. The leadership resists distraction and stays focused on the long-term mission.

7. Time and Trust from Shareholders

Even the best compounding investment cannot unfold its potential unless shareholders are willing to stay the course. A true compounding machine is a company that rewards long-term thinking. You should see that management communicates clearly and that the company's story remains intact, even during short-term setbacks. The power of compounding only works when given enough time. Great companies make it easy to hold on.

How can you recognize such a company?

Ask yourself:

- Can this company double in size over the next five years—and do it again after that?

- Is it growing faster and more profitably than its competitors?

- Is it becoming more dominant over time, rather than less?

- Would I trust this CEO to manage my family's money for the next thirty years?

If you can answer these questions with a yes, you may have found a true compounding machine. And if so, you don't need ten other stocks. You just need to hold on to this one—long enough. Compounding machines turn time into wealth. They don't require brilliance or luck. What they need is time, patience, and clarity. Once you identify a true compounding engine, the power of exponential growth will take over. A stock, held long enough with the right ingredients, is not a bet. It's a formula.

It's worth noting: very few companies meet all of these criteria. But there's a good chance you already know the right one— and are familiar with its products or services.

Let's now summarize the key characteristics of a stock that can make you a millionaire. You can recognize it by three essential qualities:

1. A long-term growth perspective

- Is the market still in its early stages?

- Are there opportunities for growth over decades?

- Has the company only realized a small fraction of its potential?

2. A sustainable competitive advantage

- Does the company have a real moat?

- This could be brand strength (like Apple), network effects (like Meta), superior technology (like Nvidia), or cost leadership (like Amazon).

3. Founder-led or visionary leadership

- CEOs who think in decades, not quarters

- Bold decisions with a clear mission

- A focus on innovation, not short-term gains

In the following section, we will explore these three traits in more detail.

Find a Company That Can Grow
for Decades

If you want to put all your capital into a single stock, you need more than just a good product, strong financials, or a powerful brand. You need a company that can develop and grow steadily over many years—ideally, for decades. That's because the power of compounding only unfolds over time—and time requires room to grow.

But what exactly does "growth potential" mean? A company with long-term growth potential operates in a massive target market, has a scalable business model that becomes more efficient with each additional customer, possesses deep innovation capacity to expand into new markets, and has enough runway to grow revenue and profits consistently—not just for a few quarters, but for many years.

The key isn't how fast a company is growing today, but how long it can continue to grow. This is crucial for the one-stock portfolio. If you hold only a single stock, compounding becomes your greatest ally. But a company that grows for only two or three years offers only short-term gains. One that can grow for 15 or 20 years builds real wealth.

You need a business that doesn't simply hit a ceiling—it keeps finding new markets or consolidates its dominance in existing ones. So how do you recognize true long-term growth potential?

There are four key traits to look for when identifying a company with extraordinary long-term growth prospects:

1. A massive and expanding total addressable market.

Ideally, the company is still early in its development—perhaps it has reached only 5 to 10 percent of its potential market. It becomes even more attractive if the business model can scale globally. Take today's growth frontiers, for example: Cloud computing—with providers like AWS or Microsoft Azure—is still in its early stages of worldwide adoption. In artificial intelligence, companies like Nvidia or Palantir are just beginning to unlock the true scope of applications. And in electric mobility and energy infrastructure—consider Tesla—a whole new system still needs to be built. In other words, the market isn't just growing; it's still being created.

2. A scalable business model

The crucial question is: Can the company serve more customers without a proportional increase in cost—and even improve margins as it scales? Software businesses like Adobe, Salesforce, or Microsoft are prime examples. A product is developed once and sold millions of times, without significant additional production costs. Streaming platforms like Netflix show how content can be distributed globally with minimal added expense. In such businesses, growth and scale go hand in hand.

3. A strong pipeline for innovation and new markets

It's not enough to have succeeded once. The best companies continuously evolve, rather than resting on past achievements. Amazon started with books but now dominates global e-commerce, cloud services, logistics, advertising—and increasingly, healthcare. Apple, once focused solely on computers, has continually reinvented itself through the iPod, iPhone, Apple Watch, digital services, and now the Vision Pro. The idea is not just to ride existing trends, but to create new paths for growth.

4. Global applicability of the business model

Can the company roll out its products or services internationally—or is it tied to local market conditions? Platform businesses like Uber, Airbnb, or Spotify show how scalable models can be deployed across borders. Traditional retailers, by contrast, often struggle to replicate their success in new markets due to differences in culture, logistics, or consumer habits.

Looking at industries with particularly long growth runways helps identify promising one-stock portfolio candidates. Artificial intelligence is still in its infancy across nearly all sectors. Cloud computing benefits from digitization and the exponential rise in data. Renewable energy is a global megatrend driven by decarbonization goals. Semiconductors underpin nearly every future technology. Biotechnology and healthcare are poised to grow as the global population ages and personalized medicine advances. Electric mobility and energy storage are central to the future of transportation and power. Fintech and digital payments are reshaping the financial system as a whole. All these sectors have one thing in common: They offer vast markets, strong scalability, and the potential for durable competitive advantages—ideal conditions for building a one-stock portfolio.

Find a Company with a Strong Economic Moat

Warren Buffett popularized the term "moat" to describe a company's sustainable competitive advantage. But what exactly is a moat—and why is it so crucial when selecting a stock? The metaphor comes from the protective trenches surrounding medieval castles: the wider and deeper the moat, the harder it is for attackers to breach the walls. Applied to business, a strong moat protects a company's business model from competitors and ensures it can continue defending—or even expanding—its market share, profit margins, and earnings over time. If you're putting all your capital into a single stock, you want to be certain that the company can't easily be copied or displaced. A moat provides:

- Pricing power
- Customer loyalty and repeat business
- Long-term visibility and planning
- Stable or growing profit margins
- Resilience against competitors and crises

In short, a company with a strong moat is far more likely to grow for years or even decades—and that's exactly what you need to build exponential wealth. Let's take a closer look at the different types of economic moats.

1. Network Effects

The more users a product has, the more valuable it becomes for everyone. Examples include *Facebook* (Meta), *Instagram*, or *WhatsApp*. Since 2012, Meta stock has delivered gains of over 1,600%. Other examples include *Snapchat* or, in China, *WeChat* (Tencent). Network effects are also found in platforms and marketplaces like Amazon, *Etsy* (focused on handmade and creative goods), or *Alibaba*—companies most people know and use.

Network effects are also present in mobility and the sharing economy. Well-known names include *Uber, Lyft*, and *Bolt*. The more drivers join the network, the shorter the wait times—and the more attractive the app becomes for users.

In food delivery, *DoorDash, Delivery Hero*, and *Just Eat* are clear examples. More restaurants mean more users, and more users make it harder for new players to enter the market.

Another strong example: payment networks and fintechs like *Visa* and *Mastercard*. The more merchants accept them, the more attractive they become for cardholders—and vice versa. The same applies to *PayPal*: merchants offer it because many customers use it, and customers use it because many merchants accept it. In the past 15 years, Visa stock has returned over 3,000%, while Mastercard has delivered over 5,000%. Why consider a company with strong network effects? Because every new user increases the value of the network for all others—

creating a self-reinforcing loop that competitors struggle to break.

2. Brand Power

Brand strength is one of the oldest and most powerful economic moats. Companies with strong brands enjoy the trust, loyalty, and willingness of customers to pay premium prices—even when cheaper or technically equivalent alternatives exist. Brand power means customers aren't just buying a product—they're buying into a brand. These companies sell not only features but a feeling, an identity, a promise—and that leads to pricing power. Customers accept higher prices, and loyalty remains strong despite competition.

This also creates a "perception monopoly": in certain categories, there's only one brand in the customer's mind. On top of that, these companies benefit from a high level of trust—customers believe in the brand's quality before even trying a new product.

The textbook example is *Apple*. Customers willingly pay high prices for iPhones, even though more affordable Android alternatives exist. The Apple brand stands for design, quality, and status—not just technology (even though Apple excels here as well). The result: loyal users and record-breaking profit margins.

Another classic example is *Coca-Cola*. Though nearly identical to *Pepsi* in product, Coca-Cola feels different. The brand is globally associated with refreshment, tradition, and joy—and it's been the undisputed market leader for over a century. Notably, Coca-Cola has long been one of Warren Buffett's favorite stocks. He's held it for decades and, as of March 2025, owns 400 million shares. In 2024 alone, his fund earned $776 million in dividends from this position.

Another strong example of brand power is *Nike*. Nike doesn't just sell shoes—it embodies the motto: "Just Do It." The brand represents athleticism, performance, and self-motivation. Athletes, influencers, and pop culture amplify this image— Nike is the brand of movement.

Louis Vuitton (LVMH stock) is another well-known case. Luxury thrives on brand strength. Many products command high margins because the logo is worth more than the product itself. When you buy a brand from LVMH, you're purchasing prestige, belonging, and exclusivity. In this case, the brand *is* the product. Over the past 15 years, the LVMH stock has delivered returns of over 2,000%.

Why is brand power such a formidable moat? First, it shields a company from price wars. Branded products are less price-sensitive—customers willingly pay more. Profit margins often remain stable, even in crises. Brand loyalty tends to last decades. An Apple customer often stays with Apple, even if rival products are technically superior. Entry barriers for new competitors are high—you might replicate the product, but not the brand. Brands are built over years through marketing, experience, and emotional association. This leads to lower marketing costs per sale. Well-known brands don't need to explain themselves—recognition drives sales. Word of mouth and trust often replace traditional advertising.

How do you recognize a company with brand power? Ask yourself: Would I be willing to pay more just because of the logo? Do I know someone who identifies emotionally with the brand? Is the brand name synonymous with the product itself (e.g., "to google," "Kleenex," "Velcro")? Does the company have a compelling story that sets it apart from competitors?

If you answer yes to these questions, it's likely the company is protected by brand power—making it a strong candidate for a one-stock portfolio. In a world where products grow increasingly similar, the brand becomes the true differentiator. Companies with strong brands don't just have customers—they have fans. And fans come back—and pay more. Again and again. Brands create trust, and trust builds wealth. For you, as a long-term investor, that means predictable revenues, stable margins, and a durable moat.

3. Technological Advantage / Patents

A technological moat exists when a company is so far ahead of its competitors that it would take years to catch up. This lead may come from research, patents, proprietary data, hardware, software, or a combination of all these. Technology may be invisible, but its effects are enormous. A company with a technological edge can innovate faster, operate more efficiently, deliver better products—and dominate a market others may want to enter but simply cannot.

When is a technological moat in place? When a company's technology is objectively superior, difficult to replicate, and positioned to maintain or widen its lead. This type of moat functions like a technological monopoly—even when no legal monopoly exists. Rapid innovation creates a lasting lead. A company that is already ahead today will only widen the gap through continuous improvement. Competitors try to catch up, while the leader pulls further ahead. With each year, the company develops new features, systems, and data advantages—raising the barriers to entry. It often commands better margins, either through pricing power or operational efficiency. Technology leaders can charge more—or produce at lower cost.

One of the best-known examples is *Nvidia*. The company is the global leader in graphics processors (GPUs)—critical for AI, gaming, and data centers. It holds a decades-long lead, especially in AI acceleration. Proprietary software platforms like CUDA further deepen this moat.

Another strong example is *ASML*. It is the sole manufacturer of advanced EUV lithography machines used in chip production. Without ASML, cutting-edge semiconductors wouldn't exist— even Intel, TSMC, and Samsung rely on them. ASML stock has also returned over 1,000% in the past 15 years.

Another company with a significant technological edge is *Palantir*. Palantir develops data analytics platforms—originally for intelligence agencies. It holds a technological advantage in the visualization and integration of complex data sources.

Technological advantage doesn't mean a flashy, short-lived product. It's not about being "cool." It's about sustained technological dominance that may last decades. You can copy a smartphone, but not the entire Apple ecosystem. You can build an electric vehicle, but not Tesla's software or battery management systems. Anyone can build a chatbot, but not one trained like OpenAI's language model—on billions of data points.

So how do you recognize a technological edge in a company? Ask yourself: Does the company own platforms, systems, or patents that are hard to replicate? Does it benefit from data-driven network effects (the more users, the better the product becomes)? Is there a clear and ongoing focus on research and development? Is the company a critical partner for competitors or governments? Has it proven its superiority across several generations of products?

Technology can become outdated, but a true edge endures. Not every tech company has a technological moat. But if one does, it acts like an invisible wall that protects the business from competition. In fact, this is the only type of moat that tends to deepen over time, not weaken. For a long-term investor, this is crucial: a company that leads its industry through innovation has the best chance at sustained exponential growth—and is therefore an ideal candidate for a one-stock portfolio.

4. Cost Leadership and Economies of Scale

Now let's talk about cost leadership and scale advantages— true economic moats. A cost-leading company can offer its products or services at lower prices than competitors, without sacrificing quality—and sometimes even improving it. This moat is structural. It becomes stronger with each additional unit sold. The bigger the company, the more efficient it becomes, and the harder it is for others to catch up. That's the essence of economies of scale: declining unit costs as production volume rises. Companies that reach this point early lock in a significant long-term advantage.

What does cost leadership look like in practice? It means the company can produce more cheaply—through automation, supply chain dominance, or bulk purchasing power. It can price aggressively to gain or defend market share. Alternatively, it can maintain higher margins even at lower prices. Either way, it puts pressure on less efficient competitors. Cost leadership isn't luck—it's the result of process efficiency, scale, infrastructure, and capital strength built over years.

Economies of scale mean that the larger the company, the lower the cost per unit. This includes purchasing (bulk discounts from suppliers), production (automation pays off at large volumes), fixed cost distribution (R&D, marketing, and admin spread over more units), and logistics (automated warehouses and in-house delivery networks).

Here are a few strong examples of companies with cost leadership and scale advantages:

Amazon has a vast logistics infrastructure—own warehouses, airplanes, and drivers. It operates its own cloud business (AWS) and benefits from the scaling of its digital infrastructure. Amazon can offer lower prices without sacrificing margin.

Walmart is another example. Its massive purchasing power allows it to negotiate better supplier prices and pass those savings to customers—while remaining profitable.

Taiwan Semiconductor Manufacturing Company (TSMC) also benefits from huge economies of scale. As the world's leading contract chip manufacturer, TSMC's scale allows it to make capital-intensive technologies (like 3nm chips) profitable—something smaller competitors simply can't match, even if they have similar capabilities.

Netflix is a case everyone knows. As more users stream globally, the cost per user for content production, servers, and software declines. Netflix scales across more than 190 countries. New shows can be marketed worldwide—without additional production costs. Over the past decades, the stock has returned an astonishing 42,000%. And the story isn't over.

Cost leadership gives companies a decisive pricing advantage—without sacrificing margins. They can lower prices to outcompete rivals without incurring losses themselves. Scale strengthens this advantage further: with each step of growth, the cost advantage expands. Companies with cost leadership are also far more resilient during downturns. Those with low costs are better equipped to survive price wars, supply chain disruptions, or declining demand. This also creates a capital barrier for potential challengers. New entrants would need to invest billions to reach comparable efficiency—something that rarely succeeds.

How can you recognize a company with cost leadership? Ask yourself: Does the company have a dominant market position with clear volume advantages? Are gross margins stable or even improving despite low prices? Are there signs of automation, vertical integration, or process superiority? Is there evidence that competitors cannot keep up without incurring losses? Is the company becoming more efficient year after year, rather than more complex?

A great case study is *Amazon* versus traditional retailers. Amazon locates, packs, and ships products from automated warehouses in seconds—often with same-day delivery. A brick-and-mortar retailer, on the other hand, must pay for staff, rent, inventory, and local advertising. Amazon can deliver faster and at lower cost—often with better margins. That's economies of scale and cost leadership in action. A company with genuine cost leadership wields an economic weapon that systematically weakens competitors. It grows in good times and survives the bad through efficiency. With each passing year, it grows stronger—not more vulnerable. If you're looking for a stock to hold for decades, cost leadership combined with scale is one of the most dependable and economically anchored moats—ideal for a one-stock portfolio.

5. High Switching Costs

High switching costs are often the invisible glue of a business model. A company with high switching costs doesn't lock in customers through contracts or discounts—but through complexity, effort, or risk involved in switching to a competitor.

The more difficult, expensive, or risky the switch, the stronger the moat. These types of moats are common in B2B models, but also found in consumer-facing digital platforms, software ecosystems, and services.

What exactly are switching costs? They include all the friction that makes changing providers difficult—technical setups (like software or interfaces), time spent on training, migration or integration, and the potential loss of stored data, operational knowledge, or familiar workflows. Not to be underestimated is the fear of disruption, downtime, or even the psychological comfort of sticking with the known. These hurdles often lead customers to stay, even if better or cheaper alternatives exist. The current provider is "good enough," and switching feels too costly.

Why are high switching costs considered a moat? They create stable, long-term customer relationships. Clients often remain for years, even when better solutions arise. This makes revenues predictable—ideal for planning and scaling. Since customers are not quick to switch, companies can introduce moderate price increases over time. Margins improve without high churn. This low customer attrition is a powerful advantage. In the software world (especially SaaS), a low churn rate is one of the most important drivers of long-term success. The "lock-in effect" even increases with time: the longer a customer stays, the more of their operations, data, and expertise become tied to the provider. The older the relationship, the higher the switching costs.

There are many examples of companies with high switching costs. *Microsoft* is a classic one: businesses use Office, Teams, Outlook, SharePoint, Azure—everything is integrated. Switching to Google Workspace or another provider would be technically and organizationally complex.

SAP is another example. Its software is deeply embedded in the core operations of large enterprises—from logistics and finance to HR. Switching would take months or even years, cost millions, and carry significant risk of downtime. As a result, many companies stay with SAP for decades, despite the existence of viable alternatives.

In creative software (Photoshop, Premiere, Illustrator), *Adobe* remains the industry standard. Designers and artists have built their workflows, libraries, and expertise within the Adobe ecosystem. Switching would lead to lost productivity and steep learning curves.

A provider like *Intuit* (e.g., QuickBooks) stores years of financial data for its users—switching is not just difficult but, in many cases, legally and operationally burdensome. This kind of business model is ideal for generating recurring revenue with high customer loyalty—a fact reflected in Intuit's steadily rising stock price.

How do you recognize high switching costs in a stock? I would ask the following questions: Is the solution deeply embedded in the customer's workflow? Are there historically grown dependencies on the provider (such as data, processes, or training)? Is switching associated with cost, uncertainty, or significant transition effort? Do customers stay for many years, even when cheaper alternatives exist? Are contracts or subscriptions regularly renewed with almost no cancellations?

A fitting example is *Salesforce*. Salesforce is a market leader in customer relationship management (CRM). The platform is complex, modular, and deeply integrated into sales processes. Many companies build custom tools, dashboards, and APIs on top of it—switching would be like performing open-heart surgery. The result: high customer retention, recurring revenues, and strong pricing power—reflected in the performance of Salesforce stock. Over the past 15 years, it has delivered nearly 7,000% gains, making it an outstanding candidate for a one-stock portfolio.

A company with high switching costs benefits from an invisible glue that holds customers in place—even without a contract. The business becomes predictable, scalable, and profitable. The deeper the integration, the stronger the lock-in. The stronger the lock-in, the more reliable the returns. For your one-stock portfolio, this means predictable revenue, low churn, high return on capital, and true long-term resilience. A company with such a moat is not a flash in the pan—it is a rock-solid foundation for wealth-building.

Do any companies combine all five types of moats?

One such company is *Apple*—the ultimate moat business. Apple is among the rare few that combines all five classical moats with extraordinary strength:

1. Brand Power

   Apple owns one of the strongest brands in the world. The logo stands for design, quality, status, and lifestyle. People pay premium prices even when cheaper alternatives are available. Apple customers aren't just users—they're fans. The emotional bond is immense.

2. Network Effects

   The more people use Apple devices, the better the experience becomes: iMessage, FaceTime, AirDrop—these only work within the Apple universe. Once you're in, you don't want to leave. The entire ecosystem—iPhone, Mac, iPad, Watch, AirPods—feeds itself.

3. Technological Advantage

   Apple develops many key components in-house, such as its own chips (M1, M2, A17) with industry-leading efficiency and performance, as well as its own operating systems (iOS, macOS, watchOS), all perfectly integrated with the hardware. Built-in security and privacy protections further strengthen its edge. Most competitors cannot match this level of control.

4. Cost Leadership & Economies of Scale

   Despite its premium image, Apple benefits massively from scale. It achieves high margins through mass production. The sale of millions of devices drives down per-unit costs. Software, services, and the App Store scale with minimal incremental cost.

5. High Switching Costs (Lock-In)

Switching from Apple to Android or Windows is painful. You lose access to iCloud, App Store purchases, Notes, iMessage, photo libraries, AirDrop, and more. Migration is technically possible, but emotionally and practically burdensome. Most users stay in the system because leaving feels like a downgrade.

In addition, Apple has another rare advantage: *vertical integration*. Apple controls hardware, software, design, chips, services, retail stores, accessories, and its App Store—a closed ecosystem. This strengthens all five moats even further, like a fortress within a fortress.

Apple is a textbook case of what happens when a company combines multiple moats. It's also one of the most convincing candidates for a one-stock portfolio. It's no coincidence that Apple stock has risen over 9,000% in the past 15 years. Many investors have built their wealth on the back of this one company.

The Founder and the Visionary – When the Head Becomes the Company

One of the most important reasons a long-term investor chooses a stock is often not the product, not the industry, and not even the market—it's the person at the top: the founder or visionary leader. A company led by someone deeply connected to its mission operates on a different frequency. It thinks further ahead, acts with greater conviction, and is more committed to building the future.

Take Apple, for example. The products are undeniably excellent. But many investors were drawn in because they believed in *Steve Jobs*—not just the iPhone. Jobs was the assurance that the next big thing would not only be imagined but delivered. In such cases, it's not just the product that inspires confidence—it's the vision and the will of a person who lives and breathes their company.

Visionaries don't think in quarters; they think in decades. While Wall Street obsesses over margins and next-quarter earnings, visionaries ask different questions: Where do we want to be in ten years? What technology must we build today to remain relevant tomorrow? What decision is right, even if it pays off only years down the road? This kind of thinking often creates tension between market expectations and entrepreneurial conviction. While analysts wait for the next earnings report, the visionary is already operating in a different time zone. And that's exactly how companies multiply in value—and how investments become fortunes.

A classic example is *Jeff Bezos*. For years, Amazon was criticized for not delivering profits. But Bezos remained committed to his strategy: growth before profit. He built infrastructure, launched Prime, and developed AWS—long before these investments paid off. Today, Amazon is far more than an online retailer. It's a cloud provider, logistics giant, platform, and tech powerhouse—all because a founder had the courage to invest while others hesitated.

Elon Musk is another emblem of this mindset. When he joined Tesla, electric vehicles were a fringe topic. Losses were high, skepticism widespread. But Musk thought bigger: he built batteries, factories, software, and AI. He didn't say he was building a car—he said he was building the future of transportation.

Why does this matter to you as an investor?

Because when you invest in a one-stock portfolio, you should think like a founder yourself. You're not looking for a company that delivers a strong quarter—you're looking for one that will be worth many times more twenty years from now. You don't want leadership that chases analyst expectations— you want leaders who invest even when the market doesn't yet understand. That's how compounding works. That's how wealth is built.

Visionaries don't move to the rhythm of the market. They make decisions that are uncomfortable today but create lasting value tomorrow. They invest in research, infrastructure, and people. They are builders, not caretakers. They operate with deep personal conviction—and often with skin in the game. That is, they own a meaningful stake in the company they lead. Their decisions affect not just shareholders, but their own wealth.

Bezos owned 10–15% of Amazon for many years. Elon Musk holds more than 10% of Tesla—and far more of SpaceX. Mark Zuckerberg controls over 50% of Meta through his voting shares. When a founder is that deeply tied to the company, they think differently—and act differently.

You could say that a founder gives a company its soul. They shape a culture that outlives them. They attract better talent, drive innovation, and set lasting standards. And they are willing to take risks that may take years to pay off—but when they do, they pay off massively. *Jensen Huang* at Nvidia is a powerful example. He bet on AI chips early—when the market didn't even exist. Today, Nvidia leads the world.

How can you tell if a company is led by someone like this? Ask yourself a few simple questions: Is the CEO deeply committed, or just a temporary manager? Does he think in years, not quarters? Does he own a meaningful stake in the company? Has he made decisions that were unpopular at first but paid off in the long run? Does he articulate a clear and credible vision?

If you can answer yes to those questions, you may have found a company with the potential to be your one-stock portfolio— and a leader who treats your capital as if it were their own.

Industries That Create Billionaires

If you want to build a one-stock portfolio, you need more than just a good idea. You need a company that can grow—not just over quarters, but across decades. It must be scalable, resilient, profitable, and able to reinforce itself over time. Such companies are rare, but not invisible. You don't have to hunt for secret stock tips. Many of the best compounding machines are hiding in plain sight—within three of the most powerful sectors of the global economy: technology, healthcare, and consumer goods.

Technology – Unlimited Growth Potential

No other sector has created more wealth over the past three decades than technology. Why? Because software, data, and digital platforms scale globally—often with near-zero marginal costs. Technology knows no borders, no closing times, no warehouses. Once a company leads in this space, it tends to stay ahead, thanks to network effects, lock-in mechanisms, and platform dynamics. What sets successful tech companies apart are high margins, recurring revenues, strong customer loyalty, and clear technological leadership.

The leading names (note: not investment advice) are well known:

- Apple – ecosystem, brand, scale, pricing power

- Microsoft – cloud, productivity software, enterprise integration

- Nvidia – dominant in AI infrastructure, expanding its technological lead

- Google (Alphabet) – search, ads, YouTube, Android, AI

- ASML – controls the global semiconductor bottleneck (EUV machines)

Healthcare – Innovation Meets Necessity

Healthcare isn't driven by trends, but by needs. People get sick regardless of economic cycles. An aging global population and rising chronic illnesses create strong structural tailwinds—combined with remarkable innovation in genomics, diagnostics, and therapies. In this sector, look for companies with protected know-how, regulatory advantages, scalable platforms, and robust pipelines.

Some current leaders (not investment advice):

- UnitedHealth Group – dominant in insurance and care (vertically integrated)

- Novo Nordisk – market leader in obesity and diabetes treatment

- Johnson & Johnson – diversified across pharma, devices, and consumer health

- Eli Lilly – megatrends in obesity and neuroscience

- Thermo Fisher Scientific – the world's largest supplier for scientific research (the "picks and shovels" model)

Consumer Goods – Quiet Giants with Daily Cash Flow

While tech attracts the spotlight, consumer goods companies often generate steady, predictable returns. These firms rely on familiar brands embedded in daily life. What becomes a habit is rarely questioned. The toothpaste, coffee, or subscription you use daily translates into continuous revenue. And here too, some of the most successful companies (not investment advice) include:

- Procter & Gamble – household products with global reach
- Coca-Cola – iconic brand, distribution dominance, pricing power
- Nestlé – vast portfolio in food, coffee, and health
- Costco – loyalty, scale, and membership-driven growth
- LVMH – luxury moat, pricing power, and timeless demand

Why do I recommend starting your search within these three sectors? Because technology, healthcare, and consumer goods are not just large—they are proven. These are industries with companies that can scale, whose products are used daily, that won't vanish when the market gets jittery, and that have the power to reinvest profits rather than merely pay them out. An ideal one-stock portfolio candidate stands at the intersection of growth and stability. It doesn't just sell the next big thing—it sells the next necessary thing. It is globally in demand, has a strong culture, financial durability, and leadership that thinks in decades.

Your goal isn't to find something obscure. Your goal is to find something great—something that grows with the world, protects its edge, rewards you year after year, and gets better the longer you own it. Look for a company that's necessary, not just new. Something people need today—and will need even more tomorrow. Something that endures.

If you're wondering where to begin: look around where you spend your time and money every day—where you consume, connect, search, or shop. That's where greatness often begins.

The Role of Network Effects and Monopolies

In a competitive market, companies fight for every single customer. They lower prices, pour money into marketing, and chase ever-thinner margins. But now and then, a rare type of company emerges—one that doesn't just compete, but dominates. Not because it's aggressive. Not because it got lucky. But because its structure gives it an unfair advantage. These companies benefit from network effects and evolve into monopolies or quasi-monopolies—making them ideal candidates for a one-stock portfolio. Let's explore how they work, and why they can become true wealth-building machines.

What Are Network Effects?

A network effect occurs when the value of a product or service increases with the number of users. The product becomes more valuable—not because the company improves it, but because the network itself grows. The classic example is the telephone. One person with a phone is useless. Two people create a use case. A hundred people form a network. A billion people turn it into indispensable infrastructure.

Today, many of the world's most valuable companies rely on digital network effects: size creates value, which attracts more users—leading to even more size. When network effects take hold, a flywheel begins to spin: More users increase value.

More value attracts more users. More users make it harder for competitors to catch up. Margins improve as scale increases, and the company becomes a standard platform. This creates exponential growth and a monopoly-like economic position— even if regulators don't officially define it as such. The more people use the product, the harder it becomes to live without it.

A clear example in recent years is *WhatsApp*. It's used by billions globally, and countless family and social groups now rely on it for communication. You're practically forced to install the app if you want to stay connected.

Sometimes, network effects involve two interacting user groups. A good example is *Uber*: more drivers attract more riders; more riders, in turn, attract more drivers. Or *Airbnb*: more hosts attract more guests, and more guests attract more hosts.

The same logic applies to *Visa* and *Mastercard*: the more merchants accept the cards, the more consumers use them— and vice versa.

More usage also improves the product itself—through better algorithms and personalization. Think of *Google*: the more people search, the smarter the search engine becomes. Or *Spotify*: recommendations improve based on listening behavior. Or *Facebook*: the more activity, the more the algorithm learns to boost engagement.

What About Monopolies?

A monopoly isn't just about controlling a market. It's about setting the standard. Legally defined monopolies are rare.

But practical monopolies—where one company becomes the default choice—are widespread among today's corporate giants.

The hallmarks of these monopoly-like businesses: massive market share, scale advantages, pricing power, and no real alternatives. Brand dominance plus network effects create the standard.

These companies aren't inherently anti-competitive. Often, they win because they're faster, cheaper, better integrated, or more user-friendly. That makes them practically unbeatable.

Examples of network-effect monopolies include:

- Google (Alphabet): 90% global market share in search
- Facebook (Meta): 3 billion monthly users across its apps
- Visa & Mastercard: global payment infrastructure
- Apple: ecosystem lock-in and network effects across devices, services, and apps
- Amazon: millions of buyers and millions of sellers in one place
- Microsoft (Office/Azure): the enterprise standard for productivity tools

Why Are These Moats So Powerful?

Because they create self-reinforcing dominance. Network effects and monopoly dynamics lead to:

- Accelerating user growth
- Rising profitability through scale

- High switching costs and customer retention

- De facto industry standards

- Long-term resilience against competition

For a one-stock portfolio, these are the rare companies that can build wealth over decades—not just quarters. Their structural advantages don't just protect their lead—they deepen it over time.

Competitors Can't Keep Up Without Massive Capital

New market entrants can't attract users without an existing user base. The product improves even as costs remain flat. Revenue scales while marginal costs fall. That's what makes these companies ideal engines for the power of compounding. You don't just own a great business—you own a self-reinforcing system that becomes better, bigger, and more profitable over time. These companies don't merely grow—they pull away from the competition.

If you invest early in a company that's still in the early phase of its network-effect cycle and hold your shares, you can achieve extraordinary returns. $10,000 invested in:

- Amazon in 2005: worth over $1 million today

- Google at its 2004 IPO: worth over $500,000 today

- Nvidia (powered by developer and AI network effects): up more than 100x in the last 10 years

These returns weren't driven by hype, but by network-driven dominance. And importantly, you didn't need to buy at the IPO or during the early years to benefit. All of these stocks could have been purchased at multiple points over the past 15 years—and still delivered exceptional gains.

If you want to hold a stock for decades, it should have four defining traits:

- Longevity

- Growth

- Competitive defensibility

- Optionality (capacity for new products or services)

Companies with network effects and monopoly dynamics check all of these boxes. They're not just businesses—they're ecosystems. Once you're in, you tend to stay. And once a company has taken the lead, it tends to stay on top.

Network effects and monopoly dynamics are rare, powerful, and exponential. You should aim to invest in a company that gets stronger with time and scales without needing constant new capital. It's an investment that protects itself.

That's why I'd look specifically for a business whose value increases with every new user—and whose market position resembles a fortress, not a battlefield. If you find a great company with network effects and hold it long enough, it can become your personal monopoly on wealth.

Why You Should Buy the Market Leader

In business—and in investing—the winner doesn't just get a slice of the pie. The winner takes almost everything. When it comes to building serious, life-changing wealth through investing, a clear pattern emerges: the companies that dominate their market or sector don't just perform well—they outperform massively. In nearly every industry, the market leader captures the majority of profits, attracts the best talent, enjoys the strongest customer loyalty, and—crucially for investors—delivers the highest returns. So if you're building a one-stock portfolio, there's one non-negotiable rule: choose the winner. Not the sector. Not the theme. Not the top five. Choose the *leader*—and let that company lead your portfolio.

Let's explore why market leaders win big—and why betting on them isn't just smart, but essential. A market leader isn't just a company with high revenues. It's the company that sets the rules, defines the customer experience, and becomes the standard others must follow. Market leaders benefit from:

- Brand trust: Customers buy what they know

- Scale advantages: Bigger means cheaper, faster, more efficient

- Network effects: More users create more value, attracting more users

- Talent magnetism: Top talent wants to work for the top brand

- Pricing power: Customers are willing to pay more because they believe in the brand

- Investor confidence: Easier access to capital, stock issuance, and growth initiatives

The more dominant a market leader becomes, the harder it is to catch. Consider these giants who have turned dominance into generational wealth for investors:

- *Amazon* (e-commerce & cloud): The leader in online retail and cloud infrastructure (AWS), with unmatched network, logistics, and tech advantages. Early shareholders became multimillionaires.

- *Apple* (consumer tech): Dominates high-end markets with iconic products—iPhone, App Store, AirPods, Apple Watch—that strengthen each other through vertical integration and ecosystem design.

- *Google/Alphabet* (search & digital ads): Over 90% global market share in search. Its data and ad dominance power massive profits and feed its AI advantage.

- *Nvidia* (GPUs & AI): The undisputed leader in AI hardware with a growing ecosystem—well ahead of competitors in both tech and market mindshare.

The competition can't catch up. These companies are too far ahead—technologically, operationally, and in brand perception. Market leadership translates into exponential pricing power. They haven't just survived—they've pulled away from the pack and used their scale to widen the gap.

One common mistake investors make after "missing" the market leader is buying the runner-up instead. But in sectors like tech, retail, social media, cloud, or semiconductors, the second-best company often captures only a fraction of the value. Ask yourself: Would you rather own Google or Bing? Amazon or Walmart? Meta or Snapchat? Apple or Samsung? The long-term stock charts speak for themselves. Even with similar revenues, profits and pricing power flow to the leader. In markets driven by network effects, scale, and platform dynamics, the winner often takes all—or most.

There's another reason to bet on the market leader: credibility. Leaders attract analyst coverage, become household names, and appear "safer" to institutional investors. Even if that safety is partly an illusion, it drives capital into the stock, inflates valuations, boosts liquidity, and makes it easier for the company to raise and reinvest funds. It creates a flywheel: the more dominant the leader becomes, the more dominant it remains.

Market leaders are capital magnets—and compound interest loves capital. Leaders often combine multiple economic moats: brand, scale, network, intellectual property, capital, and data. As the business grows, these moats reinforce each other.

Take Apple. Its brand attracts top developers, which strengthens the App Store, which boosts iPhone sales, which deepens customer loyalty, which attracts even more developers. It's a self-reinforcing system—one that smaller competitors struggle to break into.

If you want to build your future around a single stock, you need to ask yourself: Is this company the leader—or just one of many players in the space? If you own the market leader and have the discipline to hold it long enough, you don't need diversification. You only need to be right once.

So if you're serious about long-term wealth, don't spread your capital across a handful of "pretty good" companies. Find the one that stands above the rest—in fact, find the *best company in the world*. And don't make the mistake of thinking you're too late. Warren Buffett, famously, didn't invest in Apple until 2016. By then, Apple had already risen more than 14,000% from its dot-com lows. Late to the party? Maybe. But that didn't stop Buffett. Even though the chart looked stretched, Apple became his single best investment of all time. Since 2016, the stock has climbed another 1,000%. And as of April 2025, the story is far from over.

There's another crucial reason to buy the market leader—not the runner-up: all the major funds and institutional investors buy the leaders. When the smartest money in the world is buying the same handful of companies, that's not a coincidence. If you study the 13F filings of the world's top hedge funds, pension funds, sovereign wealth funds, endowments, and mutual funds, you'll notice a striking pattern: they all seem to own the same dozen stocks:

- Apple
- Microsoft
- Amazon
- Google (Alphabet)
- Nvidia
- Meta
- Berkshire Hathaway
- Visa
- Johnson & Johnson
- UnitedHealth
- Broadcom
- Salesforce

You might ask: "Why don't these funds diversify into 200 lesser-known companies? Why are they all betting on the same giants?"

The answer is simple, rational, and revealing: *because the market leaders win.* And the big money knows it. Smart money wants one thing: risk-adjusted returns. Major investors aren't chasing thrills—they're after predictability, long-term earnings, capital efficiency, and massive scale. They demand management discipline. In short: they want to own the best business models in the world—those that generate enormous free cash flow and eventually return capital to shareholders.

They invest in companies that grow profits decade after decade. And those characteristics are found most reliably in category leaders.

As an investor, you need to understand: large funds can't afford to bet on small, fragile companies. If you're managing a $10 billion pension fund, a $500 billion sovereign fund, or a $3 trillion index-tracking ETF, you can't park serious capital in tiny, illiquid stocks with high risk. Why?

The reason is simple: *position size*. These capital-heavy funds can't take meaningful stakes in small caps without dramatically moving the price. They need to be able to enter and exit positions without disrupting the market. This is one of the reasons why market leaders rarely "crash" like smaller stocks sometimes do. The deep pockets of large institutional investors provide built-in price support. You can see this reflected in the chart patterns: these stocks typically move in steadier trends. Every dip is met with fresh inflows of capital. And from personal experience, I can tell you—that's a comforting feature when you're holding a one-stock portfolio.

Another reason why large investors cluster around market leaders: their own stakeholders don't want to see speculative or obscure names in the portfolio. They demand transparency, reporting standards, and corporate accountability. So what do these institutions do? They buy the best-known, highest-quality, best-performing companies—and they buy them in size.

Buying market leaders is a self-reinforcing strategy. As more capital flows into the same set of winners, prices steadily rise—often independent of short-term news. Volatility declines, making the stocks even more attractive to other funds. Valuations stay strong because demand is constant. These stocks become "core holdings" for ETFs and index funds. The compounding continues because capital drives growth, buybacks, and innovation. It creates a powerful feedback loop: great companies attract capital. Capital makes them stronger. Stronger companies deliver better returns. Better returns attract more capital. Market leaders become wealth machines—not just for individuals, but for entire institutions.

One of the great ironies of so-called "passive" investing is that it's not neutral at all—it's highly concentrated. The S&P 500, for example, is weighted by market cap. This means the top 10 companies make up 30% or more of the entire index. Who are those top 10? The same market leaders: Apple, Microsoft, Amazon, Nvidia...

So when 401(k) contributions flow into index funds, when sovereign funds buy U.S. equities, when robo-advisors invest for Millennials—all that capital flows into the same handful of stocks. This institutional dynamic creates persistent demand for the leaders, regardless of macroeconomic conditions or daily sentiment.

If all the major players—armed with research, experience, capital, and discipline—are buying and holding the winners, ask yourself: Why shouldn't you? Why try to outsmart the smartest money in the world by doing the opposite?

That's why I say: *Follow the money.* Own what the world's best investors own. But do it with conviction—and concentration. The one-stock portfolio simply takes institutional wisdom to its logical conclusion: If the smartest investors in the world buy the market leader—but only assign it 2–5% of their portfolio— why not make it 100%? Why not take their best idea—and make it your only idea?

Part 3: How to Buy the Right Way

Time in The Market Matters Far More Than Timing the Market

One of the most common questions new investors ask is: "When is the best time to buy?" Many people wait for the perfect entry. They try to catch the lows and avoid the highs. They study charts, hoping to pinpoint the "ideal moment." But ask the world's greatest investors and they'll tell you: it's not about timing the market. What matters far less is *when* you invest—and far more is *how long* you stay invested. In other words: the real key to building wealth isn't predicting the next correction or rally. It's staying invested long enough for compound interest to work its magic.

Timing means buying low and selling high—trying to guess bottoms and tops. But anyone with experience in the stock market knows that it's nearly impossible to do that consistently. Even professional traders admit they're wrong about entry points more than 50% of the time. How they still manage to make money despite that is something I explain in my trading books. But here, the goal is different: to build lasting wealth by holding a single outstanding stock.

Time in the market means staying invested through multiple cycles. It means holding a great company for many years, ignoring short-term volatility, and letting compound interest do the heavy lifting. Unfortunately, most investors get it completely wrong: they're obsessed with entry points and overlook the real engine of wealth—the long-term ownership of a compounding machine. What do the numbers say? Let's compare two investors, each starting with $10,000:

Investor A buys a great stock (like Apple, Amazon, or Nvidia) at a "bad" time—right before a temporary decline. But they stay invested for 20 years.

Investor B tries to time the market. They only buy after the stock has corrected 30% or more, but they constantly buy and sell. They never hold for more than 3 to 5 years.

Now let's apply this to two investors who both buy Apple:

Investor A invests $10,000 at Apple's peak before the financial crisis—in 2007. Seventeen years later, that investment is worth around $900,000.

Investor B buys in March 2009—perfect timing, the low after the 2008 crash. But they sell after just three years, and their investment is worth only $60,000.

Even though Investor A bought at the worst possible moment (Apple dropped over 60% after its 2007 high), they let time do the work. Investor B had the perfect entry—but not the right exit. And as every experienced investor knows, money is made not at the *entry*, but at the *exit*. That's a truth most investors fail to understand. The outcome is clear: Investor A ends up far ahead—despite "bad timing." Why? Because time *in* the market matters far more than timing the market.

The real risk isn't buying at the wrong time—it's failing to hold long enough. Great companies are not flashes in the pan; they often need decades to realize their full potential. Timing may feel smart and safe—it gives the illusion of control. But in reality, it leads to missed compounding and emotional decisions, which means self-doubt and underperformance. Plus, frequent timing incurs extra taxes and fees. The biggest threat to your wealth isn't poor timing—it's being unwilling to stay invested.

The fact is: humans are bad at timing. Our brains are wired for action. When markets fall, we want to *do* something. When they rise, we fear missing out. We crave control—but the market almost always rewards patience. The deeper problem with timing is this: the biggest returns often occur in very short windows. Miss just the ten best days in a decade, and your returns could be cut in half. And here's the twist: those ten best days usually come right after the worst ones. So if you sell in fear, you'll likely miss the rebound. Great investors like Warren Buffett don't try to time the market. Buffett simply buys exceptional businesses—and holds them for decades.

> *"Our favorite holding period is forever."*
>
> *Warren Buffett*

Peter Lynch put it this way:

"No one can predict interest rates, the future direction of the economy, or the stock market. Dismiss all such forecasts and focus on what's actually happening in the companies you own."

If you've chosen an extraordinary company—one with long-term growth potential, visionary leadership, and global reach—then the best time to buy is *today*. The smart move isn't to find the perfect entry point, but to hold long enough for exponential growth to unfold. Time multiplies. Timing distracts. The market rewards those who stay the course—not those who jump in and out based on headlines, tweets, or forecasts.

So don't waste your energy searching for the perfect entry. Instead, find a great business, start investing—and stay invested, even when things get rough. Let time and compounding do the heavy lifting for you.

Should You Invest All Your Money at Once?

Investing all your money at once—also known as a lump-sum investment—means putting your entire capital into your chosen stock immediately, rather than spreading it out over time (as with dollar-cost averaging). While this approach may feel emotionally risky, especially in a volatile market, there are strong mathematical and strategic arguments in its favor—particularly if you truly believe in the stock you've selected. Here's why:

1. More Time in the Market = More Compound Growth
   The biggest advantage of a lump-sum strategy is this: compounding begins immediately. Every day you wait is a day your capital isn't working. If your stock grows at 20% annually, then every month of hesitation costs you real returns. For example: if you invest €100,000 today at a 20% annual return, you'll have around €619,000 after 10 years. But if you spread that investment over 10 months—€10,000 each month—the bulk of your capital is delayed. Your end result could be 10–15% lower after 10 years. The key insight: the sooner your money is invested, the sooner compounding can do its work.

2. Data Supports Going All In
   Numerous studies (e.g., by Vanguard, Schwab, Morningstar) show that lump-sum investing outperforms

dollar-cost averaging in about 70% of cases over long time periods. Why? Because markets tend to rise over time. Waiting for the "right moment" often means missing gains. This is true even in volatile markets—because the math of time beats the emotions of timing.

3. Conviction Builds Commitment

If you've done your homework and truly believe in the company, the business model, the leadership, and the competitive edge, then going all in shows conviction— not recklessness. You're saying: "I've made my decision. I'm investing now." This clarity makes it easier to stay calm during volatility—because you're no longer second-guessing or waiting for a better entry.

4. Simpler Psychology

Ironically, spreading your investment over time can increase anxiety. You keep asking: "Should I buy this month, or wait?" You risk missing major moves and experiencing FOMO (fear of missing out). Every price fluctuation becomes a source of stress. A lump-sum investment gives you mental closure—you've made your move and no longer need to make twelve nervous little decisions. One bold move is often easier than a dozen hesitant ones.

5. Better Alignment with the One-Stock Strategy

The one-stock portfolio is about clarity, focus, deep conviction, and long-term belief in compounding. If you're confident that this is the right decision, then a lump-sum investment reflects your thesis. Dollar-cost averaging is a strategy for uncertainty. A lump-sum is a strategy for clarity. If you know what you want—why wait?

That said, there are good reasons not to invest everything at once. A lump-sum approach isn't for everyone. You might consider dollar-cost averaging if you're emotionally sensitive to price swings, if the stock is highly volatile or speculative, or if you're unsure about the valuation or timing. Going all in is not about market timing. It's about trusting your process, your research, and your conviction. If you've found an exceptional business and your goal is long-term wealth creation, a lump-sum investment typically offers the longest time horizon, the clearest psychology, and the greatest upside potential. In the next chapter, we'll take a closer look at the alternative: dollar-cost averaging.

Dollar-Cost Averaging – The Smart Way to Build a Stock Position

While going "all in" with a lump sum may seem bold—and sometimes is—there's a powerful alternative strategy that offers psychological safety, emotional discipline, and statistical resilience: *Dollar-Cost Averaging (DCA)*. This method involves investing equal amounts into a stock at regular intervals, regardless of the current price. In this chapter, we'll explore how DCA works, when and why it can outperform a lump-sum investment, and how it might perfectly align with your conviction in a single stock.

DCA ensures that you automatically buy more shares when the price is low, and fewer when the price is high. Over time, this can lower your average cost per share—especially in volatile markets. The goal is not to time the market. It's to build your position steadily and without emotion. While lump-sum investments can be more profitable in hindsight (particularly in rising markets), they carry greater risk. If you invest all your capital right before a correction or bear market, your position might remain underwater for years—even in a great company. A steep drop right after a major purchase can cause fear and self-doubt, often leading less experienced investors to panic-sell, undermining their entire strategy and the power of compounding.

But there's an even more important reason to consider DCA: Many investors freeze, waiting for the "perfect moment"—and end up not investing at all.

That's one of the most common mistakes: seeing the opportunity but failing to act. DCA removes the pressure to pick the perfect entry point. It also turns investing into a habit. Each month, you invest a set amount into your stock—no matter what the market is doing. Many fortunes have been built this way.

DCA also helps smooth out volatility. You buy through ups and downs, averaging out price fluctuations. In turbulent markets, DCA often leads to a better average entry price than any single purchase. It also strengthens emotional discipline. You don't have to "time" the market or wait for a long-anticipated correction. You simply follow your plan—reducing fear, greed, and hesitation. Your investment becomes a system, and that's a powerful advantage. DCA is process-driven, not outcome-dependent. It's about long-term behavior—not short-term prediction.

And importantly, DCA keeps you invested while you build conviction.

At the beginning of your journey, you may not feel ready to invest everything at once. DCA lets you build your position gradually, while continuing your research, observing the business, and deepening your confidence.

If, for example, you save a portion of your salary every month, DCA is the natural investment method. Here's a practical example using Amazon stock:

Let's say you want to invest $12,000 in Amazon starting in January 2010.

- Option A: Lump-Sum Investment
  You invest the full $12,000 in January 2010. By 2020, the value of your investment has grown to over $200,000.

- Option B: DCA (12 x $1,000 per month)
  You spread your investment across each month of 2010. By 2020, your investment is worth $215,000.

In this case, DCA outperformed the lump-sum investment because Amazon was volatile in 2010, and DCA allowed you to buy more shares during pullbacks at lower prices. In most cases, a lump-sum investment outperforms the DCA approach during a strong bull market. However, the reality is that markets do not move in straight lines. In the case of volatile stocks with long time horizons, DCA often wins—not just financially, but emotionally. And that emotional aspect is crucial. After all, you're going to be emotionally invested if you plan to put your entire available capital into a single stock. You'll watch every move the stock makes (whether you should is a different matter...). Unfortunately, the constant availability of real-time stock prices today makes long-term investing harder, not easier. Just imagine a time when you had to wait until the next day's newspaper to see your stock's closing price. You'd have no idea what happened during the day. Wouldn't that be a much more peaceful way to build wealth? The sad reality is that many investors panic-sell their stocks during irrational market drops (which happen quite often). If the market rebounds the next day and you've already sold your position, regret can hit hard. That's why I recommend DCA for most investors—even if they have the full investment amount ready from day one.

Dollar-Cost Averaging works best when the stock is volatile but fundamentally strong, and when you're receiving new funds over time—whether through saving or other sources. It's also a great strategy to avoid overthinking and under-investing. Being under-invested is one of the biggest issues in the market. Many people experience occasional big wins, but they only committed small amounts—so the success barely changes their financial picture. And that's what truly matters. That said, even with DCA, you can build a meaningful position over time. There's often a psychological hurdle between "I believe in this company" and "I'm ready to make it my largest investment." DCA helps bridge that gap. With DCA, your conviction and your capital can grow together.

And by the way—it doesn't have to be an either/or decision. You don't have to choose between DCA and a lump sum. You can combine both strategies. For example: invest $1,000 per month as your base plan (DCA). If the stock drops by 20%, add a one-time bonus investment. This is something smart, experienced investors often do. Because they follow their stock closely, they can recognize when a one-time opportunity arises. That way, they combine discipline with flexibility—a truly powerful mix.

Building a concentrated position doesn't have to happen quickly. It can unfold over years. What matters is that it happens deliberately. Dollar-Cost Averaging is the quiet superpower of the focused investor. If your goal is to hold a world-class company for five, ten, or even twenty years, then how you enter the position is less important than staying in it. In the end, you'll realize something surprising: The timing of your entry matters far less than you'd think. Imagine your stock is now trading at $80, and your first purchases were at $14. Does it really matter whether you bought at $14 or $17? The answer is no. What matters most is that you bought—and stayed invested—through the journey to $80. That's what counts.

So it's perfectly fine if you're not ready to go all in. Just take it step by step, month by month. Let math—and the business— do the rest. Look at the long-term (monthly) charts of the great stocks mentioned in this book or on your brokerage platform. You'll see it often didn't matter whether you bought the stock today, tomorrow, or next month. If you've found a true winner, steady investing is often more powerful than a single bold move.

The Right Charts for Long-Term Investors

Charts are powerful tools. They allow us to visualize price trends, spot long-term patterns, and better understand a stock's behavior over time. Unfortunately, many investors use the wrong kind of charts for long-term investing. They zoom in too closely, become obsessed with short-term movements, and rely on tools designed for traders—not investors. If you're building a one-stock portfolio, you need a different mindset. Think in years, not days. Focus on compounding, not on green or red candlesticks. You don't need a microscope—you need a map.

Use weekly or monthly charts—not daily charts. Daily charts are for traders. They're noisy, showing every small move, every gap, every flicker. While helpful for day traders or swing traders, they create a false sense of urgency for long-term investors and exaggerate volatility. They make small movements seem like big problems, prompting reactions to noise rather than to meaningful signals. Weekly charts are made for investors. They smooth out the chaos and reveal the true trend, not the temporary turbulence. The benefits are obvious: Weekly charts reduce emotional overreactions and help you stay invested during corrections.

I often go even further—I use *monthly charts*. Monthly charts offer maximum clarity. They illustrate growth over time and are ideal for identifying major cycles and understanding the compounding of your capital visually. Monthly charts soothe your emotions during temporary drawdowns, making short-term selloffs appear insignificant in the bigger picture.

"If you think in decades, don't look in days."

Another key point: *Use logarithmic charts—not linear ones.*

What's the difference? Linear (arithmetic) charts represent price changes in absolute terms. Every dollar of movement looks the same. Logarithmic charts, on the other hand, show price changes in percentage terms. A move from $10 to $20 (100%) looks the same as from $100 to $200 (also 100%)—even though one is a $10 move and the other is $100.

Why do linear charts mislead long-term investors? Early gains look tiny—even if they were massive in percentage terms. The power of compounding becomes invisible. That's why logarithmic charts are essential. They show the real development of a stock over time. They allow you to view multi-decade charts in a meaningful way and help you understand how a $10 stock became a $500 stock. They also put drawdowns and rallies into proper context. When it comes to long-term investing, compounding is what matters. Compounding is an exponential phenomenon—and your charts should reflect that. Take Amazon as an example: From 2001 to 2025, the stock (split-adjusted) rose from $0.27 to $242.

Figure 9: Amazon 3-Month Chart, 2001–2025, Linear Scale

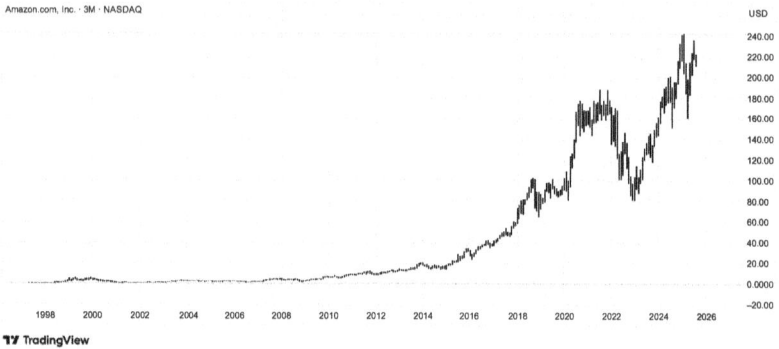

Amazon.com, Inc. · 3M · NASDAQ — USD

In the linear monthly chart, the early gains are nearly invisible. The price action looks flat until 2015, and the drawdowns in 2022 and 2025 appear massive—though in reality, they weren't.

Figure 10: Amazon 3-Month Chart, 2001–2025, Logarithmic Scale

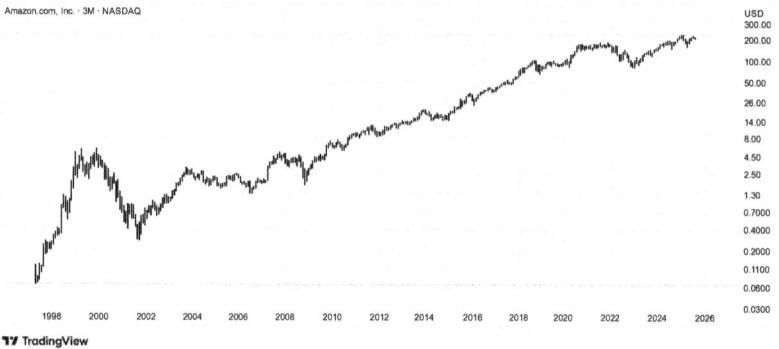

Amazon.com, Inc. · 3M · NASDAQ — USD

Now look at Amazon on a logarithmic chart—an entirely different picture emerges. The early gains are clearly visible. The 2022 and 2025 corrections appear relatively modest and even look like attractive buying opportunities. Had you relied only on linear charts, you might have missed the trend or sold too early.

The right charts reduce the urge to constantly check your portfolio or your stock, because you're now thinking in years—not hours or days. When your stock drops 20% in a single week, panic is a natural response. We'll see this in the Amazon example from August 2024:

Figure 11: Amazon, Daily Chart May–Nov 2024, Linear Scale

In this example, Amazon's stock experiences a sharp drop between July 11, 2024, and August 5. It loses more than 24% in a short period. Anyone looking only at the daily chart might easily panic. But on the logarithmic weekly chart for the same period, the drop appears as a minor blip within a strong long-term trend:

Figure 12: Amazon, Weekly Chart 2023–2025, Logarithmic Scale

This perspective is worth gold. It's how your one-stock portfolio can become a fortune. Let's look at this idea once more, schematically:

Figure 13: Amazon Growth – Linear vs. Logarithmic

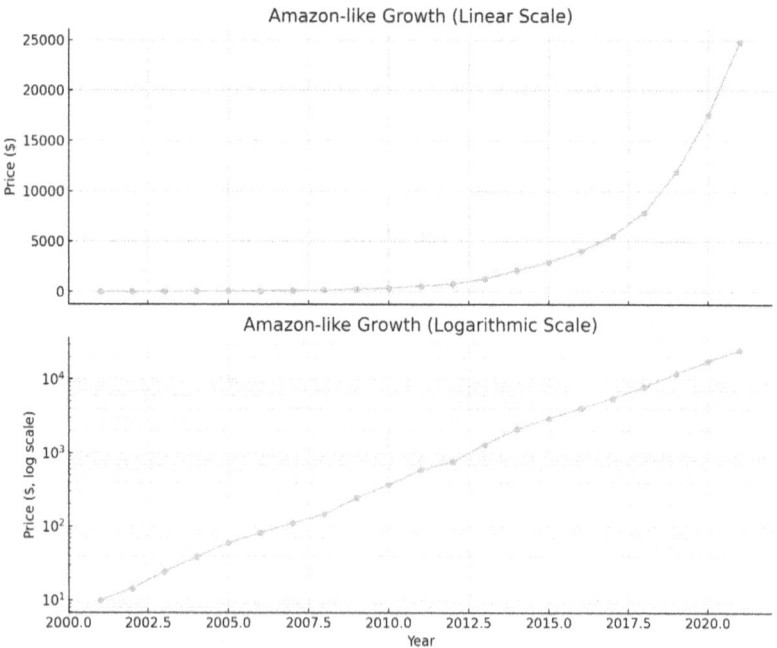

Both charts show a simulated, "Amazon-like" long-term stock performance in two different formats.

Top: the linear view – early growth looks flat, recent growth explosive.

Bottom: the logarithmic view – compounding is visible clearly and consistently across all years.

This is exactly why long-term investors should use logarithmic charts: they reflect percentage growth more accurately and help you stay rational and focused on the bigger picture.

Part 4: How to "Manage" Your Portfolio

Don't Talk to Anyone About Your Investment

The one-stock portfolio is not for nervous or timid investors. The idea alone goes against all conventional wisdom. In other words, if you want to follow through with this strategy, the main challenge will be dealing with your own psychology. The act of buying is the easiest part—it only takes a few clicks. That's why, in this chapter, we'll focus on the psychological challenges that lie ahead.

It's a fact: society conditions us to follow the crowd. We are taught to behave in ways that conform to what is generally accepted as good and right. We're expected to play it safe—taking risks doesn't fit that mold. It's no wonder this thinking also dominates most investment advice. You'll hear the same recommendations you probably grew up with—at home, in school, and later during your education or career. Most investors don't feel secure until they hold a diversified portfolio or buy the entire index—because that's what everyone else is doing. But the truth is this: if you do what the majority does, you'll end up with what the majority gets—mediocrity. Real wealth is rarely, if ever, built this way in the stock market.

Publicly, fund managers and well-known investors may preach something else. But in reality, many act exactly as I suggest in this book. It takes unconventional thinking, a certain degree of relentlessness, and even a bit of cynicism. You have to block out all the voices trying to talk you out of your plan—and there will be many. Financial media in particular are designed to scatter your attention. They push you toward a diversified portfolio and tempt you to buy a little of everything, hoping something will eventually pay off. The problem is: you lose clarity and focus. Your attention is split. You become like a circus performer trying to keep twelve plates spinning at once. It's no surprise that eventually, some of them crash.

A one-stock portfolio requires you to stand on your own in the investment world. It demands strong conviction in your choice. It also requires that you block out all the noise from the markets and the media. You must ignore the panic that arises during market corrections. And you must also ignore the doubt and disapproval from people who don't understand—or don't want to understand—your idea or your strategy.

That's why I want to give you both a serious warning and a heartfelt recommendation: *you should not talk to anyone about your investment*. I know that's difficult. It's human nature to want to share your plans and ideas. But that's exactly where social convention kicks in. You must resist the urge.

If you break this rule—which for me is an iron rule—you'll quickly find people shaking their heads. Some will even try to talk you out of it. Of course, they'll say they only want what's best for you—that's how it will be framed. I offer this advice from long experience: don't talk to anyone about your investment or your stock. Not even your spouse. Not your children, your parents, or your best friend.

That may sound harsh, but building wealth is harsh. Because you have to do something that almost no one else is willing to do. And that is the hardest part of this strategy. Not choosing the stock. Not making the purchase—that's the easy part. The real challenge is having—or developing—the inner psychological strength to stick with your decision, even when the whole world thinks you're wrong.

Don't Be Afraid of Volatility

When you hold only one stock in your portfolio, you're not just alone in your decision—you're also alone in facing the consequences. One of the greatest challenges for investors is learning how to deal with volatility: the constant ups and downs in prices. These fluctuations are a natural part of the market. Sometimes they work in your favor, but often they don't.

If you have a broadly diversified portfolio with 30, 40, or even more than 50 stocks, a decline is easier to digest. When the overall market drops by 20 percent, you can tell yourself, "This affects all of us." You're not alone. The media covers it, analysts weigh in, and there's a certain emotional comfort in going down with the crowd. A correction like those in 2022 or 2025—when the market dropped 20 percent within days or weeks—is considered normal, even healthy. Markets don't rise in a straight line. Setbacks are part of the process.

But if you hold just one stock, a correction feels very different. Even if the downturn affects the entire market, you can't blame anyone else. You face the full force of the swing alone. In those moments, fear creeps in: What if I lose everything with this one stock? That fear is real—and it becomes even stronger when you find no outside validation. No article, no analyst report, no reassuring video supports your decision. You are truly on your own.

The truth is: a 20 percent market correction feels twice as painful in a one-stock portfolio as it does in a diversified one. Because you can't say, "It's happening to everyone." It's happening to you. That's why you must be willing to live with this kind of volatility if you're aiming for extraordinary long-term returns. You can't expect a stock to go up tenfold and, at the same time, only tolerate 5 or 10 percent drawdowns. If you want 1,000 percent upside, you have to endure 30, 40, or even 50 percent declines. That's how growth works. That's how markets work. Most conservative stocks that barely fluctuate also barely rise.

Take Amazon, for example. During the dot-com crash, it lost more than 90 percent of its value. Yet it later became one of the greatest stock market winners of all time. Those who held on were disproportionately rewarded. Even in the 2022 bear market, Amazon—despite being a firmly established company—fell by more than 50 percent, twice the drop of the S&P 500. There's no guarantee that even large, well-known companies won't experience serious setbacks. Growth stocks require this kind of volatility—it's part of the game. The problem isn't the volatility itself, but the lack of willingness to deal with it.

If you're running a one-stock portfolio, you not only need to endure these swings—you need to see them as opportunities. Corrections of 20, 30, or even 50 percent are not the end;

they're often the beginning. Those who stay calm and buy when others are selling lay the foundation for substantial gains.

This is what sets successful investors apart from the crowd: the ability to remain calm when things get turbulent. Those who understand that corrections are not just possible, but likely, enter their investment prepared. And those who are prepared don't panic—they see the correction as an invitation. A one-stock portfolio demands a lot from you—but it also has a lot to give. If you can handle the volatility, if you don't panic when prices fall, and if you keep your head while others are losing theirs, you have a real shot at big success. But that takes strength. The strength to hold on when it hurts. And the clarity to realize that volatility is not your enemy—it's the price you pay for exceptional returns.

Selling Too Early – The Most Dangerous Temptation

Anyone who invests in a single stock will sooner or later face perhaps the greatest challenge of all: the urge to sell—too early. This is a common mistake driven less by rational thinking than by psychology. As soon as a stock rises significantly, the internal pressure to "lock in" profits begins to build. What seems like a sensible decision is often a costly mistake.

Imagine you buy a stock for 10 dollars. A year later, it's trading at 30. The temptation to take a 3x gain is strong. The fear of losing those paper profits can become almost physical. Behavioral finance shows that losses hurt twice as much as gains bring joy. It's no surprise, then, that many investors head for the exit—just when it would make the most sense to stay invested.

Let's return to the example of Amazon. Those who bought the stock in the early 2000s and sold after just a few hundred percent of gain missed the real move. The price development afterward was exponential—and the true mistake wasn't about risk of loss, but about the enormous opportunity cost. As mentioned before: in the stock market, it's not the losses that hurt the most. It's the missed opportunities.

One of the most common fallacies is the belief that a stock that has already risen a lot must be about to fall. Phrases like "It can't go any higher now" are among the most dangerous in the investor's vocabulary. The market doesn't care about our opinions or supposed logical limits. Companies like Amazon or Apple have risen for decades—regardless of their short-term valuation. As explained in the chapter on long-term market trends, investors consistently underestimate such trends. That goes for great stocks as well. That's exactly why we want to find a company like this—and hold it as long as possible, as if we owned 100 percent of it.

Another misunderstanding is the idea that you can sell a strong stock and buy it back cheaper later. This strategy rarely works. Once you've exited, you have to get two things right: the sale and the repurchase. In practice, many investors sell—and then wait in vain for the expected correction. Meanwhile, the stock keeps rising, and the opportunity is gone. A good entry is undone by a poor exit. When a company is growing quarter by quarter, increasing earnings and expanding market share, it is entirely possible for its stock to keep rising—even in a weak market. Those who sell during such periods risk being left behind while others continue to profit. That is the greatest risk for long-term investors: *losing their stocks*. Selling is a bet against your own conviction—and that's usually the biggest mistake.

Of course, warnings appear constantly in financial media: "This rally can't go on," "Insiders are selling," or "The stock is overvalued." Such statements are poison to any long-term investor. Those who listen often lose not only their stock but their composure. Pullbacks of 30 or even 40 percent are entirely normal—and even necessary. They are not a threat, but an opportunity. Those who have liquidity during these times can expand their position. Those who panic-sell will miss that chance.

An investor should treat the opinions of friends, acquaintances, or self-proclaimed experts with great caution—especially if they don't own the stock themselves. No one should base their investment decisions on outside opinions. It would be a grave mistake to give up a carefully built position because of a headline or analyst comment.

The list of fortunes lost to premature selling is long. Think of the early Bitcoin buyers—many owned hundreds or even thousands of coins and sold after doubling or tripling their money. We now know: with a bit more patience, many of them could have become multimillionaires. Instead, fear of giving back gains cost them their full potential. Even a simple strategy like "sell half and let the rest run" would have served them well. But fear and greed won. The biggest mistake was selling everything—and giving up the chance for extraordinary wealth.

With a one-stock portfolio in particular, the greatest gains don't come from constant buying and selling—they come from doing nothing. If you hold a true winner, don't sell it. Ever. Hold on—through pullbacks, through corrections, through chatter. Because that one stock, if it represents the right company, can change your life.

147

Signs That Your Stock Is No Longer a Winner

When you concentrate your portfolio on a single company, conviction is everything. You buy with intention. You hold with discipline. You ignore the noise and trust in the power of compounding. But there's a truth every focused investor must accept: even great companies can lose their edge—sometimes slowly, sometimes suddenly, but always with warning signs, if you know what to look for.

This chapter is here to help you identify the key signals that suggest your stock may no longer deserve its place as your financial workhorse. Because there's only one thing worse than being wrong: staying wrong for too long. A one-stock portfolio isn't about "buy and forget." It's about buying and observing. You don't react to every headline, but you're also not blindly attached to the stock no matter what. Your loyalty lies with the business, not the ticker. If the business deteriorates, you must be honest enough to reassess.

Identity investing is a psychological trap. If your one stock becomes part of your identity, you stop analyzing it critically. You surround yourself with confirmation bias and dismiss critics as "haters." You become a believer, not an investor.

Why do focused investors often miss the exit? Because when you concentrate on one company, you become emotionally attached. You lose objectivity, ignore bad news, or rationalize weak results. You start saying things like, "The market doesn't get it." You average down or double your position when you should really be reevaluating the business. The result is well known: investors ride the stock all the way up—and all the way back down. They fall in love with the idea and miss the reality. That's why mental flexibility is crucial with a concentrated strategy. Concentration isn't dangerous because of the math—it's dangerous because of the mindset.

So how do you know when your investment is turning against you? Here are some of the key warning signs that you should reconsider your concentrated bet:

1. Moat deterioration: The competitive advantage is fading
   A great company needs a wide, defensible moat. When that moat shrinks, your growth engine is in danger. Warning signs include: new competitors gaining ground quickly, customers switching to alternatives, declining pricing power, brand erosion, technological disruption, or regulatory threats.

   What to watch for: falling market share, shrinking margins, or management acknowledging "increased competitive pressure." Any decline in moat-based metrics is a clear red flag. A shrinking moat makes a stock vulnerable.

2. Revenue or margin compression

Growth is the fuel of long-term returns. If revenue stalls or margins are squeezed, compounding slows—or stops. Warning signs include: multiple quarters of stagnant or declining revenue, shrinking gross or operating margins, rising customer acquisition costs, or falling free cash flow.

Ask yourself: is the company still growing profitably—or is growth barely hanging on?

3. Capital misallocation

Even the best business can falter if management wastes capital. Watch for signs like: expensive acquisitions that don't align with the core business, large buybacks at inflated prices, excessive stock-based compensation, or declining return on invested capital.

A good business with poor capital allocation is a slow-motion wealth destroyer.

4. Cultural decay

Visionary companies are built on strong internal culture. If that culture erodes, the business may follow. Watch for the departure of founders or key leaders, high employee turnover, public scandals or reputational damage, strategic drift, or confusing product shifts.

One of the strongest warning signs: "me-too" behavior. When a company starts copying others rather than leading with its own strategy, innovation, or vision, it may have lost its edge, creativity, or confidence. Here are a few examples:

- A tech company suddenly launches a chatbot, just because everyone else is doing it.

- A consumer brand introduces a subscription model—not because it fits, but because it's trendy.

- A social media platform copies a competitor's feature (e.g., Instagram copies TikTok, or Facebook copies Snapchat).

This is the corporate version of: "We don't want to fall behind, so we'll just do what they're doing." But great companies don't act that way. They set trends, solve problems in their own way, and create unique products that reflect a clear mission. That's why "me-too" behavior is a clear warning sign for long-term investors: it points to a lack of originality, strategic uncertainty, and a leadership team that follows headlines instead of fundamentals. It marks the shift from long-term thinking to short-term relevance. In the context of a one-stock portfolio, that's dangerous. Because when a company stops leading, it starts bleeding—market share, attention, capital, and eventually returns.

5. The stock no longer responds to good news
   This one is subtle but important. If your company beats earnings, launches new products, raises guidance—and the stock doesn't move, or even drops—that can signal saturation (future growth already priced in), institutional selling, or shifting investor sentiment. When a stock stops delivering returns, it may be entering a new phase—one you might not want to stay invested in.

6. The story has changed—or disappeared

Ask yourself: Is the original thesis still intact? Is the company still as dominant as when you first bought it? Are the drivers of long-term value still in place? If the answer is "no" or even "I'm not sure," treat that as a red flag. Sample questions: Is the growth path still open? Is the moat still wide—and getting wider? Has the company become reactive rather than visionary? When the story gets blurry, the returns usually do too.

7. You start making excuses

This is the emotional red flag. You tell yourself, "It'll bounce back," or "The market just doesn't get it," or "It's only temporary" (for the fourth time in a row). "Well… it's still a great company" (even as the fundamentals deteriorate). That's not conviction—it's denial. If you find yourself defending your stock like a soccer fan defending a weak player, it's time to take a step back and get objective.

What to do when you see these signs

First of all: don't panic. Long-term investors don't sell at the first wobble. Recheck your thesis. Ask yourself: Would I buy this stock today, knowing what I know now? Focus on fundamentals—not just the stock price. A falling share price doesn't automatically mean it's a bad business. But declining margins, revenue, and profits are real.

If necessary, reduce or exit your position. Sometimes it's best to trim—or walk away—before the damage grows. Remember:

a one-stock portfolio is about clarity and conviction, not stubbornness. Being focused doesn't mean being blind. It's bold to go all-in. But staying all-in requires constant attention. Watch the business. Protect your capital. And be honest with yourself. Because in the end, the only thing worse than missing a great company is holding onto a once-great company for far too long.

When the Business Model Fails

As a long-term investor—especially one who has chosen a one-stock portfolio—your success depends entirely on the company's continued ability to make money and remain relevant. You want it to keep growing, reinvesting, and compounding over many years—perhaps decades. Great companies don't collapse overnight. They die when their business model stops working.

So first, let's ask: what is a *business model*? A business model describes how a company earns money. It answers questions such as: Who is the customer? What are they paying for? How does the company deliver value? What are the margins? How is growth reinvested?

When the model works, it creates a flywheel: attract customers – deliver value – generate revenue – reinvest in product, scale, or innovation – grow.

But when this cycle breaks down, the company begins to lose value—and eventually bleed out. The decline is often not visible at first. But under the surface, essential parts begin to erode:

1. The customer changes

Demand shifts, and new needs emerge that the company can no longer meet. The product no longer solves the right problem.

2. The value proposition weakens
   What was once special becomes a commodity. Competitors offer the same or a better product at a lower price. The company loses pricing power.

3. Margins shrink
   Costs rise, but prices don't keep pace. Economies of scale weaken, and profitability declines—even if revenue is still growing.

4. Growth becomes expensive
   Customer acquisition costs (CAC) rise sharply. Customer loyalty declines, and the company spends more just to stand still.

5. The model fails to adapt
   Leadership clings to outdated strategies. Innovation slows, and the company falls behind.

Let's look at a few real-world examples of companies whose business models eventually began to fail:

- *Blockbuster*: The old model was based on physical rental stores. The problem: the rise of digital streaming and changing consumer habits. Blockbuster failed because leadership didn't pivot in time. Result: *Netflix* took over the market.

- *BlackBerry*: The model was built on physical keyboards for corporate phones. The problem: touchscreen smartphones redefined the category. BlackBerry believed security alone would protect its position. Result: relevance and market share were lost—forever.

- *Sears:* The classic department store model offered broad selection and physical reach. The problem: the rise of e-commerce and poor reinvestment of capital. Sears failed as its assets were stripped and the online trend was missed. Result: bankruptcy.

- *Nokia*: Once the world's top mobile phone brand, Nokia missed the smartphone revolution. What went wrong? Nokia was too slow to adapt to the iPhone and Android ecosystems, relied on a clunky OS (Symbian), and the failed Microsoft partnership came too late. Leadership underestimated the speed of the platform shift. Result: the stock lost over 90% of its value between 2007 and 2012. The mobile phone division was eventually sold. Even a market leader with global dominance can fall quickly if it fails to innovate or recognize disruptive change.

- *Intel:* For years, the default choice in semiconductors. Then product launches were delayed, AMD staged a comeback, and Apple switched to its own chips. The stock stagnated for over a decade—even while the sector was booming.

- *Zynga:* The darling of "Facebook gaming." The valuation soared... then monetization failed, user numbers declined, and the hype collapsed.

- *Peloton:* The perfect stock for the pandemic year of 2020. Explosive growth, strong brand, recurring revenue model. But the surge in demand proved unsustainable. Peloton overbuilt its inventory and showed weak leadership during the crisis. It lacked a real competitive advantage beyond brand and hardware. From a peak of $160 in early 2021, the stock fell below $10 within two years. Hype does not equal durability. The stock benefited disproportionately from a one-time event (the pandemic). A great product does not necessarily make for a great business model.

In all these cases, the product still existed. What failed was the model behind it—the way the company created and captured value.

What happens to the stock when the model breaks down? At first, often very little. The stock may fluctuate. Investors stay optimistic. Management might issue upbeat guidance. But eventually, the fundamentals catch up. You begin to see earnings misses, lowered forecasts, executive departures, negative cash flow, and declining valuations—even on "good" news. In short: the real story emerges, and the market reprices the stock, often harshly.

What should one-stock investors watch for?

If you're investing in a single company, you must become the watchdog of the business model. Ask yourself regularly: Is the company still solving a meaningful problem? Are margins and reinvestment rates intact? Is customer loyalty still strong? Are competitors catching up? Is management adapting—or clinging to the past? When the model fails, everything else—brand, vision, even company culture—begins to erode.

Now the question arises: Can a company recover when its model is failing?

The answer: sometimes. A broken business model doesn't necessarily mean the end of the company. But recovery requires a radical reinvention—often new leadership, painful restructuring, time, and trust.

A well-known example is *Adobe*. The company shifted from one-time software licenses to a subscription-based SaaS model. Painful in the short term, brilliant in the long run.

Another example is *Netflix*. From mailing DVDs to streaming, then to content creation, and now even gaming. Netflix has continually adapted.

These success stories are impressive—but for every one of them, ten silent deaths follow. Keep that in mind. When your stock shows signs of needing a new business model, the odds are usually poor. The chance that management pulls off a successful pivot is slim. A stock is only as strong as its model. In the one-stock portfolio approach, you're not just betting on a product or a CEO. You're betting on a system that sustainably creates value. If that system breaks down, you must be clear-eyed enough to act. Watch the flywheel. Watch the customers. Track the margins. And above all, respond when the model starts to creak. Because a broken business model is like a broken engine: the car might still look good—but it's not going to take you anywhere.

Alternative Exit Strategies – Holding Instead of Selling

Before we explore alternative ways to make use of a position rather than selling it, let me tell you a story. A few years ago, I met an 86-year-old baron who lived in a 16th-century castle. The encounter happened by chance: I knew his housekeeper, a resolute woman who managed everything related to the estate. She lived in a small cottage at the edge of the castle grounds, with a view of the entire property from her kitchen. A bell above the door would ring whenever someone entered the estate—including when I came to visit.

The baron himself was usually only present on weekends. During the week, he resided in an apartment in one of the best areas of the city. My friend, who took care of the garden and animals, had been working for him for years. She looked after two donkeys and a prize-winning pedigree dog, which she even accompanied to dog shows. Through her, I eventually met the baron in person.

This man came from an old noble family, with a lineage dating back to the 14th century. He owned several castles and estates scattered across various municipalities. On an outing, my friend showed me a dilapidated farmhouse that also belonged to the family. The 18th-century building was run-down, the roof half-collapsed, the barn a candidate for historic preservation. The last resident, a farmer, had passed away years ago.

"What's going to happen to the farm?" I asked. "It won't be sold," she replied curtly. Even though the baron had received numerous offers, he refused to sell. The property was slowly decaying—and no one in the family seemed to care. But from my friend's stories, I knew the baron discussed almost everything that occupied his mind with her. He had never married and remained a bachelor into old age. But even bachelors need someone to talk to, and so I later learned from my friend that a prospective tenant had appeared—someone willing to lease the farm for 99 years through a ground lease.

This was typical of the baron—not to sell, but to make use of what he owned. Ground leases are tax-efficient: the annual lease payments are lower than property transfer taxes in a sale and are also fully tax-deductible. The new lessee was a horse enthusiast who wanted to renovate the farm at his own expense and lease it for 99 years. After that, everything would revert to the family. This fit perfectly with the baron's mindset: keep, don't dispose.

The baron's brother thought the same way. He lived in a 16th-century city palace, hidden behind two decaying mansions. These had been standing empty for years—selling or renting them was out of the question. Only when the city forced him to renovate did he reluctantly have some work done. But even then, he remained true to his principle: ownership stays ownership. This family doesn't think in five- or ten-year investment horizons. They think in centuries. What's once been acquired remains in the family. Whether a property sits vacant or doesn't generate income is of secondary importance. The goal isn't to squeeze maximum returns from every asset—it's to preserve it and pass it on to the next generation.

Now, one might wonder what sense it makes to leave two beautiful townhouses in a prime location uninhabited. To answer that, let me return to my one-stock portfolio. Let's assume your strategy has worked, and you're sitting on a massive gain. The stock you bought at $50 is now worth $500—or more. And now comes the big question: "Should I sell?"

This is the crux of the matter: as modern investors, we often think too short-term. We want performance, cash flow, price gains—preferably right away. But we could learn a lot from those who see ownership as a responsibility to future generations. Maybe you don't need to own a castle to adopt that mindset. Maybe it's enough to view a great stock not as something to sell, but something to make use of—through dividends, appreciation, collateral for loans, or inheritance. Sometimes the best exit is *no exit at all*—but a conscious decision to keep what you own.

Selling Triggers Taxes. Selling Breaks the Compounding Cycle. Selling Feels Like Abandoning Your Best Idea. If you still believe in the company but need liquidity or income, what can you do? That's why it's worth examining alternative strategies. Because the true cost of selling is higher than you think. Selling might seem obvious once your position grows large—but it comes with drawbacks:

1. Capital Gains Taxes

   Depending on your location, you could lose 20–50% of your gains to taxes. That's years of compounding—gone overnight.

2. Loss of Future Growth

   When you sell, you stop earning returns. If the company continues to grow, you might miss the best part of the journey.

3. Reinvestment Risk

   What will you buy after the sale? You exchange one high-conviction idea for several lower-conviction ones. Selling kills your greatest strength: focus.

An alternative: *borrow* against your stock holdings. Instead of selling, you can pledge your valuable shares as collateral and access cash while avoiding capital gains taxes. This is exactly what the wealthy and major shareholders do. It's what the baron's family in my earlier story did too. They didn't sell their real estate—because they could borrow against it whenever they needed cash.

The benefits are clear: tax deferral—no sale means no tax. You gain liquidity without having to liquidate your position. Staying in the stock keeps your compounding intact. And you're free to use the funds—for real estate, a business, lifestyle, or other investments.

Of course, there are risks too—such as margin calls. If your stock value drops significantly, the lender might demand additional collateral. You'll also incur interest costs, although those are often low and tax-deductible. Be aware that this strategy is not suitable for volatile or illiquid stocks. It works best with high-quality, liquid large caps like Apple, Nvidia, or Microsoft. That's why I recommend investing only in such stocks.

Here are some common types of leverage you can use:

1. Securities-Backed Line of Credit (SBLOC)
   Offered by many brokerage firms. You borrow money (often up to 50%) against your portfolio. No sale required, and no immediate tax impact.

2. Margin Loans
   Instant borrowing via your brokerage account. Usually higher risk and higher rates than an SBLOC. Best suited for short-term, tactical liquidity needs.

3. Structured Loans / Private Banking
   Available to high-net-worth individuals. Customized loan terms with concentrated stock positions as collateral. Can result in very low interest rates (in some cases 1–3%).

So what's the takeaway?

Wealthy people rarely sell their real estate or stocks. They borrow against them—and let the assets continue to grow. Just like the two barons did with their properties.

There are also hybrid strategies: sell a little, borrow a little. There's no rule saying you must do all or nothing. A hybrid approach might look like this: sell 10–20% of your position to diversify or fund other projects, and take out a modest loan on the rest. Use the cash for real estate, private investments, or generating tax-efficient income. This gives you liquidity, reduces risk, and still leaves room for future upside in your core holding.

When is selling appropriate?

Selling isn't inherently bad—it's just final. There are times when it's absolutely the right move. You should sell if your investment thesis is broken (the business is deteriorating, the moat is shrinking). Or if you've reached your personal financial goal—for example, financial independence.

Another reason might be to reduce risk—especially if the position now makes up 90–100% of your net worth, and you want to diversify for estate or legacy planning. But even then, I would consider selling gradually over quarters or years to reduce tax and timing risk. The key is to exit strategically—not emotionally. You're managing a growing fortune, not a lottery ticket.

If your one-stock portfolio has grown dramatically, don't think of it as something you need to "cash out." Think of it as owning a growing business—or a 16th-century castle, like in my story. It generates future earnings, can be leveraged, and becomes a financial foundation—not just a trade. If you believe in the company, treat it like a bank, not a slot machine.

As you can see: if your single stock has become a life-changing asset, you don't necessarily have to sell it to benefit from the wealth it represents. You can maintain your conviction and still make smart use of its value. It's even possible to grow it further for decades to come.

The best investors don't always sell their winners—sometimes, they build their lives around them. So before you hit "Sell," ask yourself: Do I need the money—or am I just seeking comfort? Is this the end of the story—or just the next chapter?

Because sometimes the smartest move isn't to cash out. Often, it's wiser to keep the flywheel spinning—and borrow the wind.

Part 5: Case Studies

How Stewart R. Horejsi Became a Billionaire from a Single Stock

Stewart R. Horejsi, a trained welding technician and graduate of the University of Kansas (1962), returned to his hometown of Salina, Kansas, after graduation to work in the family business. By the late 1970s, the company was under economic pressure. Increasing competition threatened its survival, and Horejsi began to worry. Around this time, he came across the book *The Money Masters* by John Train. It described the strategies of successful investors—including Warren Buffett. That book changed Horejsi's life. Shortly after reading it, he began buying shares of Buffett's company, Berkshire Hathaway.

His first purchase: 40 shares at $265 each—an investment of $10,600. Two weeks later, he added more: 60 shares at $295, then another 200 shares at $330. In total, he invested $66,000. Later, when the family business recovered, he continued buying. At the peak, he held 5,800 Class A shares, later reducing his holdings to around 4,300.

Chart 14: Berkshire Hathaway (BRK.A) 3-Month Chart, 1980–2025, Logarithmic

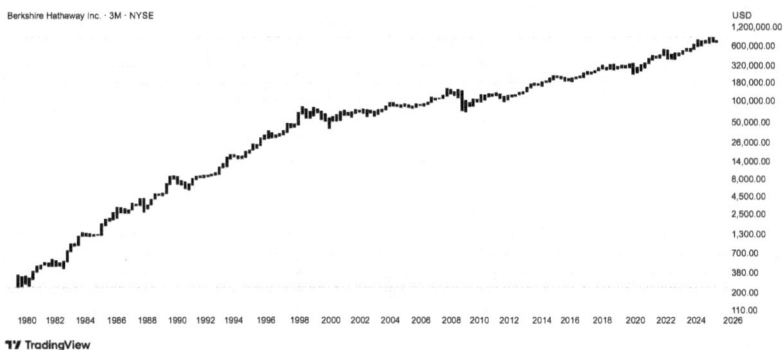

What makes this story so remarkable is that Horejsi didn't discover Buffett "early." When he started investing, the stock had already risen from $7 to $265—a gain of 3,685%. Shortly after he entered, the price reached $1,000. And still, he kept buying. Today, each of those A-shares purchased for under $500 is worth over $784,000 (as of March 2025). Horejsi's wealth is estimated at around $4.1 billion. He now divides his time between Arizona, Oregon, and Barbados—where he moved into an 18th-century plantation house once owned by Claudette Colbert. In an interview, he said of Buffett: "One of only two people who radiate an aura of integrity that you can feel the moment they start to speak."

Horejsi was by no means among Buffett's earliest investors. But in hindsight, his entry was still "early enough." Even though he had to pay a steep price at the time, that price now seems laughably low. And that's the lesson: Many investors hesitate when a stock has already risen significantly. But as Horejsi shows, investing can still pay off—even at higher prices—if the quality and vision are right.

A look at the possible performance of a $10,000 investment in Berkshire Hathaway (B-shares, since A-shares became unaffordable after 1993) vividly illustrates the kind of returns that were still possible, even with a later entry:

- Bought in 2000: 277 shares → $144,871
- Bought in 2010: 151 shares → $78,973
- Bought in 2015: 68 shares → $35,564
- Bought in 2020: 43 shares → $22,489

So, someone who invested $10,000 in 2000 (277 shares) would have seen growth of over 1,300% by 2025—even if it didn't make them a millionaire.

Is Berkshire still a one-stock portfolio candidate today?

Admittedly, the golden years of explosive growth are over. Buffett himself once said, "The wild years of Berkshire are behind us." The empire has simply become too large to sustain 20% annual growth. But an annual return of 10 to 12% is still realistic—solid, though no longer spectacular.

However, the most important takeaway from Horejsi's story is not the return. It is the determination to invest consistently— even when the stock had already risen significantly. It's the ability to turn conviction into capital. And it's the willingness to think long-term and hold when others are doubtful. What set Horejsi apart: he went "all in." His initial investment, adjusted for inflation, amounted to well over $10,000. He acted out of conviction—and that's what made him wealthy.

His story proves that even with a "mature" stock like Berkshire, long-term wealth can be built over decades. The key isn't perfect timing—it's decisive action. Those who wait for a "better" entry often miss the big picture. Horejsi didn't hesitate—he invested, held, and trusted. And he proved: one stock can be enough—if it's the right one.

Grace Groner Invested in a Single Stock for 75 Years

Grace Groner was born in 1909 in a small rural community in Lake County, Illinois. At the age of twelve, she lost her parents and was taken in, along with her twin sister Gladys, by a local community member, George Anderson. Anderson also financed her education at nearby Lake Forest College and treated her as his own child. Grace lived an extraordinarily simple life. For decades, she shared a modest one-room house with an older relative, Ann Findlay. She never married and worked for 43 years as a secretary at Abbott Laboratories—the only employer she ever had. She never owned a car, bought her clothes exclusively on sale, and regularly donated money to those in need. Her only indulgence was travel.

In 1935, she invested $180 in three shares of her employer, Abbott Laboratories. What seemed like a small investment would go on to change her life—and the lives of many others. She never sold those shares. Instead, she consistently reinvested all dividends. Over the decades, her position grew—boosted by numerous stock splits and steady dividend increases. By the end of her life, she owned more than 100,000 shares of Abbott.

Chart 15: Abbott Laboratories 3-Month Chart, 1968–2025, Logarithmic

No one around her suspected the wealth she had quietly built. After her death in 2010, it was revealed that her estate was worth more than seven million dollars. She had left it to a foundation she had established during her lifetime—with the goal of supporting students at Lake Forest College. Since then, the annual dividends of roughly $300,000 have been used to fund study-abroad programs, internships, independent research, and scholarships. The foundation's board "nearly fell off their chairs" when they learned of Grace Groner's bequest to the school.

Her entire fortune came from a single stock investment. And that one stock wasn't some speculative lucky break, but a solid business she knew as well as anyone could. Abbott Laboratories, founded in 1888 in Illinois, is a global pharmaceutical company with around 73,000 employees. The company is considered a Dividend Aristocrat—one of the firms that have increased their dividends for at least 25 consecutive years.

Grace Groner didn't trade. She didn't speculate. She didn't diversify. She simply invested, held on—and patiently watched as $180 grew into over seven million dollars. Her life was quiet, modest, and seemingly uneventful. But her example is remarkable in its message: you don't have to be a stock market guru to build wealth. All you need is discipline, long-term thinking—and trust in a strong company.

Sylvia Bloom and JPMorgan Chase

Sylvia Bloom grew up in Brooklyn as the daughter of Eastern European immigrants—during the economically challenging years of the Great Depression. She put herself through college at Hunter College and, in 1947, began working at the prestigious Wall Street law firm Cleary Gottlieb Steen & Hamilton—where she remained for an astonishing 67 years. As a legal secretary, she held a position that drew little public attention, yet it gave her deep insight into the lives and decisions of the firm's top lawyers. In an era when secretaries not only managed calendars but also handled personal business affairs, Bloom often executed investment transactions for the firm's partners. And when a partner bought a stock, she would quietly buy a few shares for herself—always in smaller quantities, given her modest salary. But she invested wisely—and she did so for decades.

One of her most successful holdings was the stock of JPMorgan Chase, which she accumulated steadily and reinvested all dividends. Her strategy was simple yet powerful: buy, hold, collect dividends—and reinvest those dividends into the same stock. This allowed her to benefit from the magic of compounding. Year after year, not only did the share price rise, but the dividends also increased—on a growing number of shares.

Chart 16: JPMorgan Chase 3-Month Chart, 1969–2025, Logarithmic

According to *The New York Times*, Sylvia Bloom built her fortune through three brokerage firms and eleven bank accounts. Despite working at one of Wall Street's most respected law firms, she lived modestly. She commuted by subway, rented a simple apartment in Brooklyn, and avoided luxury. She dressed tastefully and owned a fur coat—but it was Persian lamb, not ermine. Her wealth remained a closely guarded secret. Not even her family, closest friends, or husband knew the extent of it. When Sylvia Bloom died in 2016 at the age of 96, she left behind a fortune of $9.2 million—built entirely through quiet, disciplined investing in stocks.

The vast majority of her wealth went to charity: over $8 million was distributed according to her will. Of that, $6.24 million was donated to the Henry Street Settlement, an organization that supports disadvantaged youth—marking the largest single donation in the nonprofit's 125-year history. Two more million went to her alma mater and to an additional scholarship fund.

Even her niece Jane Lockshin, who acted as the estate executor, was stunned: "I knew Sylvia was doing fine, but I had no idea about the true size of her fortune. She simply never talked about it. For her, that was private."

Sylvia Bloom was not a star investor, entrepreneur, or analyst. She was a woman with a steady salary, a clear mind, and a quiet, persistent strategy. She bought stocks she understood—and she kept them.

The Best Stock of the Last 100 Years Was a Tobacco Stock!

1982: Frank Miller is 32 years old and working the night shift at a packaging factory in Ohio. He doesn't know much about investing—just bits and pieces picked up from *Money* magazine and diner conversations. One morning, after a double shift, he's sitting with a cigarette and a coffee, flipping through the newspaper. A small headline catches his eye: *Philip Morris increases its dividend.* Nothing dramatic—but the detail sticks. Later that same week, Frank invests almost all his savings: $5,000 in shares of Philip Morris (now Altria). No grand plan. No market timing. No elaborate analysis. Just one decision— and the patience to stick with it.

Chart 17: Altria (MO) 3-Month Chart, 1968–2025, Logarithmic

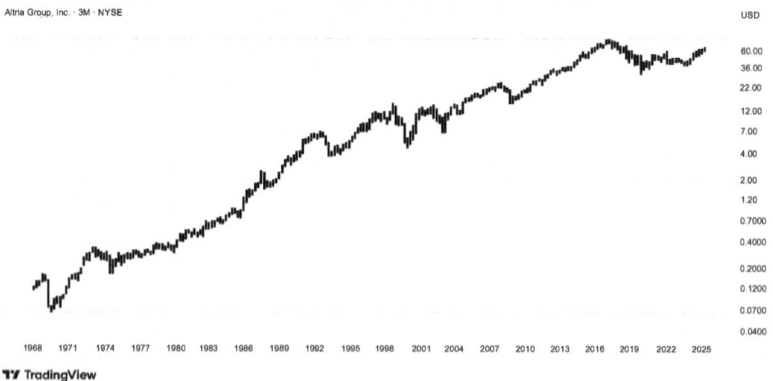

Altria Group, Inc. · 3M · NYSE

USD
60.00
36.00
22.00
12.00
7.00
4.00
2.00
1.20
0.7000
0.4000
0.2000
0.1200
0.0700
0.0400

1968 1971 1974 1977 1980 1983 1986 1989 1992 1995 1998 2001 2004 2007 2010 2013 2016 2019 2022 2025

TradingView

For years, nothing headline-worthy happens. Frank rarely checks his stock. Instead, he reinvests—quietly and consistently—every single dividend. When tobacco stocks fall out of favor, courts issue damaging rulings, and analysts call them "uninvestable," Frank remains calm: "I don't smoke the stock," he says. "I just cash the checks."

By age 50, his dividends cover half his monthly expenses. By 60, they cover everything—mortgage, groceries, fishing trips. In 2010, Frank quietly retires. His coworkers have no idea he's sitting on a seven-figure portfolio—built with just one stock. His $5,000 investment grew to over $2.5 million. All through four decades of dividend reinvestment. Frank Miller passed away in 2022, surrounded by his children. He left behind a paid-off home, a portfolio generating $90,000 a year in dividends—and a lesson he gave to his kids: "You don't have to be brilliant. You just need to own a great company—and stay out of its way."

Frank never chased the next "hot stock." He never tried to beat the market. He bought what seemed like a boring, often criticized stock—and held onto it. Sometimes, that's the key. What Frank may not have known: *he owned the best-performing stock of his time.* If you had invested just $1,000 in Philip Morris in 1970 and reinvested all dividends, by 2010 that sum would have grown to over $10 million. According to Wharton professor Jeremy Siegel, Altria (MO) was the top-performing stock in the S&P 500 from 1926 to 2010—with an average annual return of 19.75% over more than 80 years.

"The best stock of the century was a tobacco stock," Siegel writes in his book *The Future for Investors*.

Numerous studies confirm this remarkable performance. And several top-tier fund managers took Siegel's insight seriously:

- Nick Sleep & Qais Zakaria (Nomad Investment Partnership)
- Vanguard Dividend Growth Fund (VDIGX)
- T. Rowe Price Dividend Growth Fund
- Sequoia Fund
- Oakmark Funds (Bill Nygren)
- Al Frank Asset Management

They all understood: Altria was—and still is—a compounding machine. Even as cigarette volumes declined, profits kept rising. The company consistently raised prices and paid out reliable, growing dividends. While others chased tech miracles, Altria shareholders quietly collected dividend after dividend, share after share—and experienced the true magic of investing: compound interest.

Jeremy Siegel refers to this as the "growth trap"—the mistake of paying too much for supposedly high-growth companies. Between 1950 and 2003, for example, IBM traded at an average price-to-earnings ratio of 26.7, while Standard Oil (now Exxon) traded at just 13 times earnings. IBM's dividend yield was 2.18%, while Standard Oil's was over 5%. The difference? Less glamour, but more real return—year after year.

Dividends are not a nice-to-have. They're the foundation of many of the most successful long-term investments. Not because they feel "safe"—but because they produce real growth when consistently reinvested. Frank Miller's story proves: sometimes, one idea is all it takes—and the patience to do absolutely nothing else.

The Apple Man

It must have been around 2009 when I met him. I don't remember the exact date anymore. I refer to him in this book as "the Apple Man" to protect his anonymity. He is German and lives in one of those mid-sized cities that Germany has many of. He's an engineer by training and lost his job in the late 1990s due to company downsizing. At the time, he was 55 years old.

He had heard that I was involved in stock trading and invited me to lunch. The financial crisis of 2008 was still fresh in people's minds, and naturally, the conversation turned to whether the markets could recover—and if so, how. After I shared some of my own experiences during that period (I had made a notable profit with a bet on silver), he began to tell me his story.

This man had only one topic: Apple. He wasn't interested in anything else. Apparently, he had been familiar with the Macintosh since the late 1980s. He knew everything there was to know about Apple—as much as someone living in Germany could possibly know. He had memorized every detail about the company—not just from the perspective of a curious investor, but with a deep technical understanding of the operating system and its evolution. In short, he was absolutely convinced that Apple was the best company in the world.

In 1997, he had invested the rather modest severance package he received after losing his job—less than 100,000 Deutsche Marks—into Apple stock. As he admitted, this was a stroke of luck. That same year, Steve Jobs returned to the helm at Apple. By 1998, the company was profitable again, and the stock began to reflect that. The price nearly increased tenfold by the peak in early 2000. Thanks to the substantial profit he made from this investment—a high six-figure sum—he decided to "retire" and devote himself fully to being an "Apple investor." He knew he was taking a considerable risk, as he hadn't yet reached retirement age. His only "income" came from the gains he had made on his Apple bet. Still, he was confident that he could significantly grow his wealth further with this one stock.

However, part of his gains was wiped out by the bursting of the dot-com bubble in 2000. During that period, Apple's stock lost 82% of its value. He referred to this setback as tuition—what he had to pay as a still relatively inexperienced investor. He did manage to retain at least part of his original gains. But the financial pressure he was under at the time must have been immense. He was too old to start a new career, yet too young to receive a pension, which in any case wouldn't be particularly generous, since he had stopped working at 55.

The high six-figure sum he had at the start of 2000 had shrunk to a more modest six-figure amount. And from that sum, he was living.

Figure 18: Apple 3-Month Chart, 1981–2025, Logarithmic

Of course, he continued to follow developments at Apple closely. He watched the stock price, but in the early 2000s, his Apple investment was only moderately successful. He saw his capital melting away week by week like snow in the sun, due to ongoing living expenses. As he admitted to me, he had maneuvered himself into a rather uncomfortable position. On the one hand, he had some money—but not enough to retire worry-free. He was therefore forced to succeed either as an investor or as a speculator. And as everyone knows, being under pressure is one of the worst positions for making sound investment decisions.

Moreover, he refused to even consider investing in any other stock. This man was—and still is—so convinced of the uniqueness of the Apple story that he couldn't imagine putting even a single euro into anything else.

That became even more apparent when I was later invited to his home. Everything of value in his apartment came from Apple. Of course, he owned the latest iPhone. He had one of the most expensive Macs money could buy, several MacBooks, and an Apple iMac. He used iMovie, iTunes, and iPhoto. He had an iPod MP3 player, and the music he listened to came exclusively from the iTunes Music Store. He had just bought the new iPad and proudly showed it to me. In his living room, front and center, stood the latest version of Apple TV.

In short: this person had acquired every available Apple product and spent his days immersed in media from the Apple universe. If he wasn't listening to music on his iPod, he was working on digitizing old photos on his Mac—so he could view them across all his devices. When he wanted to relax, he watched TV via Apple TV. He lived and breathed Apple—and that's why he was only capable of investing in Apple stock.

His major financial breakthrough came between 2003 and 2007, when the stock rose by a staggering 3,000 percent. From 2003 onward, he kept investing more and more, until he was almost fully invested just as Apple began its next meteoric rise. By the time I met him in 2009, he had been able to realize most of his gains. He had learned his lesson during the dot-com crash and managed to preserve the bulk of his profits when the 2008 financial crisis hit, causing Apple stock to drop by more than 60 percent.

When I met him, he was already reinvested—not 100 percent, but he had once again bought Apple shares with about 30 percent of his available capital. That was what he wanted to talk to me about. He felt a bit uncertain. He had been "lucky" twice with his Apple investments, and he was honest enough to admit that he wasn't sure he could pull it off a third time. From today's perspective, that seems obvious. After all, Apple rose another astonishing 9,000 percent from its post-financial crisis low to its all-time high in December 2024.

The last I heard of the Apple Man was that he had indeed become a multi-millionaire and no longer had anything to worry about. He "made it" by investing in just a single stock for his entire life. His inability to invest in anything other than Apple shares turned out to be his greatest strength. I have never met another investor so singularly convinced of one thing as the Apple Man. For him, it was a fact: Apple was the best company in the world—and therefore, buying Apple stock was the only option. History proved him right.

Retiring with Tesla: The Story of Jason DeBolt

Jason DeBolt, a former software engineer at Google and Amazon, became a multimillionaire through his radical focus on Tesla stock. At 39, he quit his job and retired. His story is a powerful example of how much conviction, risk, and persistence a one-stock strategy can require.

His Tesla journey began in 2009. He saw the prototype of the Model S and immediately thought: "This is the future." He was fascinated by its simplicity compared to combustion engines. He ordered a car, and when he later picked it up at the factory, he was overwhelmed by the vertical integration, the degree of automation, and the technological ambition. At that moment, he realized the market was underestimating Tesla—especially in light of the upcoming Model 3.

DeBolt bought his first 2,500 shares at $7.50 each—about 20 percent of his available capital at the time. Even though Tesla was on the brink of bankruptcy, his conviction kept growing. In May 2013, he added 150 shares at $82, then another 142 shares at $141 in November. He saved everything he could and invested consistently. His last major purchase was in March 2014: $26,000 at a price of $235 per share.

Chart 19: Tesla Monthly Chart, 2010–2025, Logarithmic

To invest even more, DeBolt gave up his expensive Silicon Valley apartment and began sleeping in his Tesla—parked at Google. He used all the free facilities Google offered its employees: food, showers, laundry service, and the gym. He funneled every dollar saved on living expenses into more Tesla shares. He even tried to get a job at Tesla but never received a call back.

In late 2014, he opened a margin account to buy even more stock using borrowed money. His conviction was unshakable—but also incredibly risky. At one point, he held 25,270 Tesla shares, 10,000 of which were bought on margin. When the stock crashed in 2018, he faced massive margin calls. He was forced to sell the borrowed shares, realizing heavy losses. His takeaway: "With margin, I ended up losing money overall."

Still, he stuck with Tesla. In January 2021, his position had grown to nearly $12 million thanks to the massive price rally. At that point, he quit his job at Amazon Web Services and retired.

One of his smartest moves was rolling over $97,000 from his 401(k) retirement account into Tesla stock. That portion alone grew to over $5 million—just through buy-and-hold and reinvestment. Despite setbacks, DeBolt stayed resolute. On September 8, 2020, he lost $1.3 million in a single day when the stock dropped 21%—but he didn't sell. When Tesla's stock plummeted by 75% in 2022, he didn't panic. Instead, he sold his Los Angeles home for $3 million and bought another 10,000 Tesla shares at prices between $128 and $139. Just a few months later, in January 2023, the stock rebounded—netting him $400,000 in gains.

Today, DeBolt lives in a house by the sea and spends his time exploring philosophy and machine learning. His investment in Tesla was more than a financial decision. He believes in the company's mission, in Elon Musk, and in Tesla as a revolutionary force across energy, mobility, and technology. He still holds his Tesla shares. In his view, they could be worth between $20,000 and $30,000 each by 2030.

DeBolt once said, "Keeping my Tesla shares is more important to me than staying retired. If it really came down to it, I'd rather go back to work than sell a single share."

Andrew Hall: One Big Hit – and Why It Rarely Happens Twice

As powerful and impactful as a single big bet can be, most investors only manage such a coup once in their lifetime. If you look closely at the biographies of successful investors, you'll notice a recurring pattern: they typically became wealthy through one brilliant decision—but were unable to repeat that feat later on.

Warren Buffett is one of the rare exceptions. He built billions with multiple concentrated bets—on Coca-Cola, American Express, and Apple, among others. But outside of such exceptional talents, the reality is clear: most well-known investors owe their reputation to a single spectacular idea. Their later ventures often pale in comparison—or even fail. The golden encore rarely comes.

A striking example is Andrew Hall. In the early 2000s, he became convinced that oil, priced between $25 and $30 per barrel, was severely undervalued. He saw rising global demand—especially from China—paired with a tightening supply. Hall bought long-term oil futures with maturities of five to ten years, a risky strategy that many considered insane. But it paid off: when oil surged to over $140 per barrel in 2008, Hall made billions from his positions.

Chart 20: WTI Crude Oil Monthly Chart, 2001–2008, Logarithmic

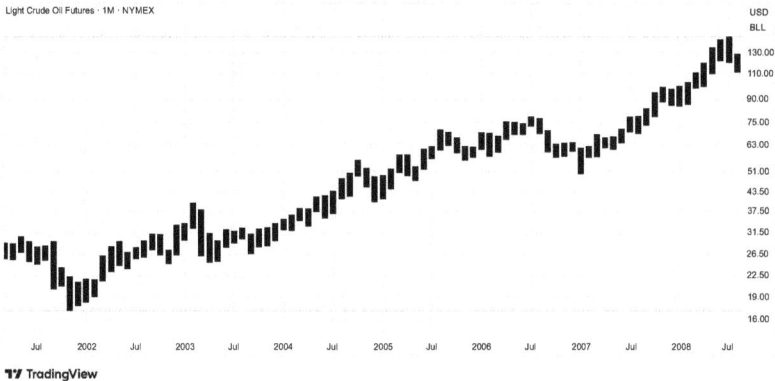

Light Crude Oil Futures · 1M · NYMEX

That success catapulted him into a different world. He moved into a medieval castle in Bavaria, began collecting artworks by Warhol and de Kooning, and even opened his own museum.

In 2010, he founded the hedge fund Astenbeck Capital—but the second success story never came. As oil prices failed to develop as expected, he was forced to shut down the fund in 2017.

So why didn't Hall pull off another big win? Was it a one-time opportunity? Or had his energy been fully spent on that first strike? Probably both. A bet of such magnitude demands extraordinary effort—emotionally, financially, and in time. For those who manage to turn modest capital into a fortune, there's often neither the need nor the drive to try again. History is full of one-hit wonders in the investing world—followed by mere "wealth management."

And that brings us to the central thesis of this book: *you only need one idea to become financially free.* One stock, one company, one market—that's all it takes. The goal isn't to find new opportunities again and again. It's to recognize the one big opportunity—and seize it completely.

Professional fund managers can't implement this approach. They have to present new ideas to clients regularly, rebalance portfolios, and avoid concentration. Most people wouldn't trust a wealth manager who put all their money into a single stock. But that's the strength of a private investor: you don't have to answer to anyone. If you have the courage, you *can* go all in.

This is a personal decision. No one can make it for you. But most investors encounter such an idea at least once in their lifetime. The real question is not: Will you recognize the opportunity?—but rather: Are you willing to act on it?

Because it takes enormous mental strength to go all in on a single conviction. The cautious won't dare. Those who listen to conventional wisdom never will. But anyone aiming for extraordinary results must take extraordinary action. It's a decision that defies typical thinking—and that's exactly why almost no one makes it.

Many investors know the feeling: "I should go all in on this." But then they talk about it. They seek validation, share their idea—and in doing so, often lose clarity. That's why my advice is: keep it to yourself. Don't talk about it, not even with your closest circle. Not because you shouldn't trust them—but because you must protect your conviction. Nothing kills bold investment decisions faster than the fear reflected in a skeptical friend's eyes.

This is also why so many great fortunes are built "in silence." No one knows until the will is read. Then it's revealed that an unassuming person did just one thing for decades—with full dedication. And that is not "normal." Someone who invests in only one stock for 30 years doesn't live conventionally—they live with focus. With a plan. With inner clarity that sets them apart from 99 percent of other investors. Such a strategy may only work once in a lifetime—but that's enough. If you follow it with discipline, you won't need to repeat it. One decision is enough to achieve financial freedom.

How Keith Gill Made Millions with GameStop

Keith Gill was born in 1986, the son of a truck driver and a nurse, and grew up in Brockton, Massachusetts. "I grew up with video games and shopping at GameStop," he said in a 2021 congressional hearing. In 2009, he graduated from Stonehill College and worked between 2010 and 2014 at a startup where he tried to develop software to help investors analyze stocks, as he later testified. Before his rise to fame, he worked in financial services, including as a Chartered Financial Analyst (CFA) at MassMutual. "My salary never exceeded $40,000, but I learned something about investing. I learned how to do the hard work of digging through a company's financials and focusing on its actual long-term value," he said.

For fun, Gill began posting investment-related content on YouTube under the pseudonym "Roaring Kitty," blending stock analysis with memes, humor, and sincerity. In mid-2019, Gill started buying GameStop (GME) shares, believing them to be undervalued and heavily oversold. At that time, GME traded around $4–5 per share and was widely dismissed on Wall Street as a failed brick-and-mortar retailer. But Gill saw more. There was new leadership (including Chewy founder Ryan Cohen joining the board), strong liquidity despite weak sales, and massive short interest—many hedge funds were betting against the stock.

He began building a position and posted updates on "WallStreetBets," where users initially mocked him. "If I'm wrong, I lose money. If I'm right, people could make life-changing gains." In September 2019, Gill—under the username DeepFuckingValue—posted a screenshot of a trade consisting of a $53,000 long position in GameStop stock. The position included shares and 500 call options. In a YouTube video, he stated that his argument did not constitute financial advice: "I don't provide personal investment advice or stock recommendations during the stream."

Chart 21: GME Weekly Chart, 2019–2021, Logarithmic

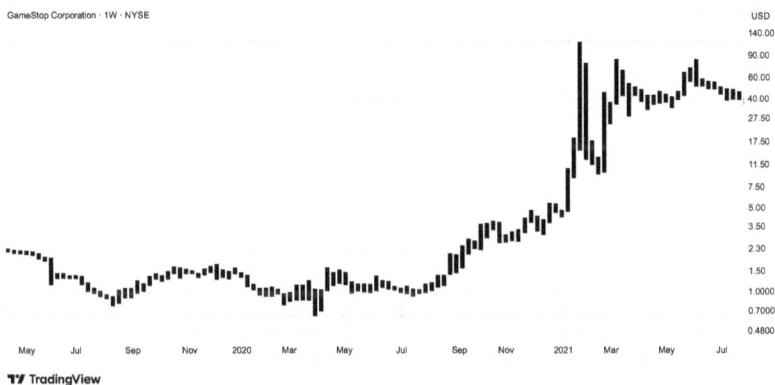

In January 2021, a perfect storm formed: Reddit users on "WallStreetBets" picked up on Gill's thesis, and traders began buying in droves. The short interest had exceeded 100% of the available float—a short squeeze became possible. Within days, the stock price exploded from $20 to over $480 per share. Hedge funds scrambled to cover their shorts, pushing the price even higher. Gill's original $53,000 investment briefly soared to more than $48 million. On February 19, 2021, he posted a screenshot showing he had doubled his GameStop holdings—now owning 100,000 shares. On April 16, 2021, he exercised all 500 call options with a strike price of $12 on the day they expired and bought an additional 50,000 shares, increasing his total position to 200,000 GameStop shares.

The dramatic surge in GameStop stock ultimately attracted the attention of regulators, the media, and the U.S. Congress. In February 2021, Gill was asked to testify before Congress—alongside the CEO of Robinhood and several hedge fund managers. In his testimony, Gill stated: "I am not a cat. I am not an institutional investor. I just like the stock." His direct, humorous defense of his investment made him a cult hero among retail traders.

On June 13, 2024, Gill posted another screenshot of his portfolio on Reddit: he held over 9 million GameStop shares worth $262 million and $6.3 million in cash. His total net worth at the time was around $268 million.

Gill's fame extended far beyond the investing community. His story inspired the Hollywood film *Dumb Money* (2023), in which he was portrayed by Paul Dano.

Keith Gill's GameStop investment was much more than a financial coup—it became a cultural moment. His success story shows what's possible when an ordinary investor does thorough research, trusts their instincts, and doesn't sell too soon.

"The most successful investors are the ones who are just a little crazy. You have to be cut from a different cloth to act that way," said Michael Khouw, co-founder and chief strategist at OpenInterest.PRO. "You would never see a professional trader achieve results like that," Khouw added. "Most of our risk managers would have intervened long before it got that far. It's simply unimaginable."

Part 6: Lessons from Failure

Examples of Investors who Failed With A Single-Stock Bet

There are numerous prominent investors—some legendary, others rising stars—who suffered major setbacks or even career-defining failures due to placing too much faith in a single stock. These stories serve as powerful reminders: concentration amplifies results—both on the upside and the downside.

One example is *Bill Ackman*, hedge fund manager at Pershing Square. He built a massive position in *Valeant*, a pharmaceutical company known for its aggressive M&A strategy. What went wrong? Valeant relied heavily on acquisitions and drug price hikes. Reports of accounting irregularities and questionable distribution practices emerged. Congressional scrutiny followed, destroying both the stock and the company's reputation. The share price plunged from $250 to $10. Pershing Square lost over $4 billion. Ackman's lesson: "We became too enamored with the company, its management, and its prospects." It shows that even the smartest investors can fall into the story trap—believing in the narrative rather than the fundamentals.

Another case is *Bruce Berkowitz*, founder of Fairholme Capital. He bet heavily on *Sears*, convinced of the value of its real estate holdings and brand under CEO Eddie Lampert. What went wrong here? Lampert focused on financial engineering instead of reinventing retail. Sears couldn't keep up with Amazon and Walmart. The business shrank, stores closed, and the brand lost relevance. Sears filed for bankruptcy in 2018. Berkowitz's fund performance collapsed: "We underestimated the pace of retail's decline."

The story of *Masayoshi Son* is also instructive. As CEO of SoftBank, Son invested over $10 billion in *WeWork*, believing in its potential to revolutionize the office space market. Why did it fail? WeWork's business model was never profitable. Leadership issues arose with founder Adam Neumann, the IPO collapsed, and massive write-downs followed. SoftBank lost billions, and its reputation took a hit. Son's mistake: too much trust in the founder, too little attention to unit economics.

Across all these cases, a pattern emerges: many of these investors believed more in the story than in the fundamentals. They held onto their positions and ignored warning signs as the underlying business deteriorated. Some placed too much trust in management without critically evaluating the results.

Personally, I see the greatest weakness in the lack of clear exit criteria. "Just hold" is not a strategy—it's inertia. Without a plan to adjust or reduce risk, you leave your capital exposed. That becomes especially dangerous when a single stock makes up 30%, 50%, or more of your portfolio—as it did in all these examples. What can we learn from this? Courage needs a brake. These stories don't argue against the one-stock portfolio—they argue for intelligent, disciplined, and adaptive concentration.

One stock can make you wealthy—but it can also ruin you if you stop thinking critically.

How to Protect Yourself Against Worst-Case Scenarios

If you go all-in on a single company—no matter how great it is—you are exposed to all the risks that affect that company: competitive disruptions, regulatory changes, earnings disappointments, market sell-offs, or Black Swan events. The advantages of concentration are clear. But the downsides can hit suddenly and with force. The solution isn't necessarily diversification, as is often claimed. The key lies in intelligent protection: using strategies that shield you from downside risks without capping your upside potential.

1. Options Strategies: Protection Without Selling

Options allow you to insure your stock holdings—much like insuring your house or car. This is called *hedging*: reducing risk, not eliminating it. The goal is to be prepared for the unexpected while still participating in upside gains. Think of it like a seatbelt: it won't prevent a crash, but it can prevent the worst. Let's say you own 100 shares. You buy a put option—the right to sell your shares at a predetermined price. For example, you buy a put with a strike price of $200 while the stock is trading at $250. If the price drops to $150, the put allows you to sell at $200—limiting your losses. Like insurance, you pay a small premium for peace of mind. The benefit: your downside is capped, but you stay fully invested. The downside: puts can be expensive and require some basic options knowledge. An alternative: use *collars* (buying a put and selling a call) to reduce the cost of protection.

2. Partial Profit-Taking and Asset Rebalancing

To secure your finances without fully exiting your position, consider selling a small portion—say 10–20%—and reallocating into other assets: cash or short-term bonds, tangible assets like real estate or farmland, gold or Bitcoin as alternative stores of value, or dividend stocks to diversify income. This builds a liquidity buffer without surrendering your winner. You're building a moat around your portfolio—without selling the castle.

3. Use Other Assets as Personal Safety Nets

You can hedge not only your portfolio, but also your life. Examples include:

- Building a cash buffer to cover 6–12 months of living expenses
- Owning rental properties
- Creating a second income stream (e.g., a small business or side job)
- Investing in skills that preserve your long-term earning potential

  These measures offer emotional and financial stability—so you're never forced to panic-sell your stock.

4. Define Mental Stop Levels Based on the Business, Not the Price

A mental hedge is a clarity tool: set predefined triggers that would prompt you to re-evaluate your position. For instance: "If revenue declines for two consecutive years...", "If gross margin falls below 30%...", or "If the founder and CEO unexpectedly leaves..." This prevents paralysis if business conditions deteriorate. It's not a price-based stop-loss—it's a company-specific fail-safe.

5. Borrow Instead of Selling (to Maintain Liquidity)

If you need liquidity but don't want to sell, consider a securities-backed line of credit or margin loan. Borrow 20–40% of your portfolio at low interest rates—avoiding capital gains taxes and keeping your compounding engine running. This shields you from being forced to sell at an inopportune time.

6. Behavioral Risk Management: Expect the Unexpected

Often, the best protection is psychological. Prepare mentally: your stock could fall 50%—even great companies do. You may watch others sell while you hold. Having a checklist for monthly or quarterly reviews can help. Conviction without discipline is just disguised gambling.

You don't hedge because you're afraid—you hedge because you're responsible. Concentration builds wealth; protection preserves it. Don't sell your winners too early. Don't panic over volatility. Instead, build smart protective layers—so your compounding engine can keep running uninterrupted. Because one stock can change your life—as long as you guard it against the few things that could destroy it.

Part 7: Alternatives to Stocks

How Much Capital Do You Need for a One-Stock Portfolio?

As you read this book, you might come to the conclusion that a one-stock portfolio is not realistic for you—either because you don't have enough capital or because you lack the patience to stay invested long enough.

The beauty of the one-stock portfolio lies in its simplicity. You focus on an extraordinary company and let time and compound interest do the work for you. The time horizon typically required for success is more than 5 to 10 years. Still, you might ask yourself: *"How much do I need to invest to make this work?"*

The answer depends on two factors: how you define success and the long-term annual return (CAGR) of the stock. Let's break it down.

Step 1: Define "Success"

Success is personal. But for clarity, let's define a few common financial milestones:

- Financial cushion: $50,000 to $100,000
- Financial flexibility: $250,000 to $500,000
- Financial independence: $1 million or more

It's up to you to decide where you want to be in 5 or 10 years. Don't underestimate what's possible if you stick with an investment over a decade. To reach these goals, we work backward: how much would you need to invest today to hit those milestones, assuming the stock delivers solid, long-term returns?

To do that, we first need to clarify what we mean by "long-term returns." We use *CAGR*—the Compound Annual Growth Rate.

CAGR answers one key question: "If my investment grew at a steady rate each year, what would that annual growth rate be?" It includes the effect of compounding—unlike a simple average return.

Why is CAGR important? It shows how fast your investment truly grows over time. It smooths out volatility and reflects the real long-term performance. It also helps you fairly compare different investments. In a one-stock portfolio, CAGR is everything. A stock that compounds at 20% per year will vastly outperform dozens of slower-growing ones.

Let's say you invest $10,000 and 10 years later it has grown to $67,275—that corresponds to a CAGR of 21%, even if the growth didn't occur evenly year to year. A stock with a 20% CAGR can completely change your life—if you give it enough time. The chart below shows how $10,000 grows over time at different CAGR levels (e.g., 5%, 10%, 15%, 20%).

Figure 22: Growth of $10,000 at Various CAGR Levels

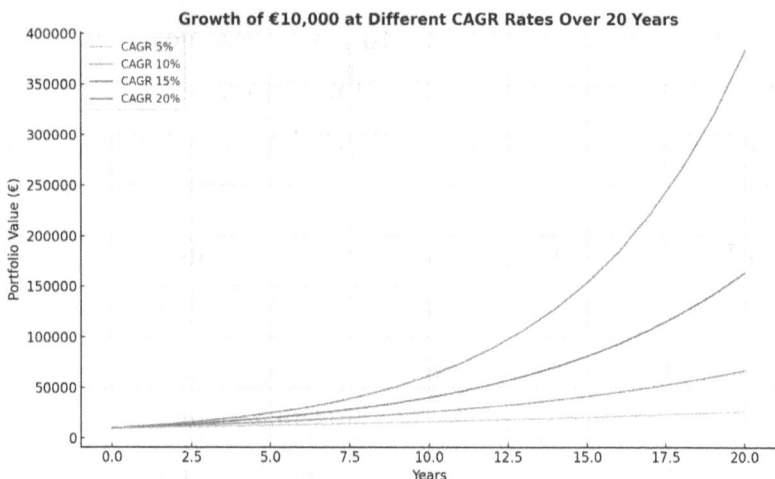

Growth of €10,000 at Different CAGR Rates Over 20 Years

As you can see, the differences become dramatic over time. From year 10 onward, exponential growth at 15% or 20% really starts to pull away from lower-growth paths.

That's why it's so crucial to understand what types of stocks are suitable for a fast-growing portfolio—and which are not. With a CAGR of just 5%, your investment barely grows after 20 years. But a 20% CAGR stock can transform your financial life.

The following section presumably lists specific stocks that have delivered different CAGR levels (5%, 10%, 15%, 20%) over the 2015–2025 period to illustrate the long-term impact of compounding.

Stocks with a CAGR of approximately 5% (stable performance with low volatility)

These companies offer moderate growth and are often attractive to conservative investors seeking stability:

- Johnson & Johnson (JNJ): A diversified healthcare giant known for consistent performance and reliable dividend payouts.

- Procter & Gamble (PG): A leading consumer goods company with a portfolio of well-known brands and stable returns.

- Coca-Cola (KO): A beverage industry leader with a long history of steady growth and dependable dividends.

Stocks with 10% CAGR (Moderate Growth Leaders)

These companies combine solid returns with growth and stability:

- Microsoft Corporation (MSFT): A technology leader with strong market presence in cloud computing and software services.

- Apple Inc. (AAPL): Known for its innovative products and powerful ecosystem, Apple has shown robust growth over the years.

- Visa Inc. (V): A global payments company benefiting from the ongoing shift toward digital transactions.

Stocks with 15% CAGR (High-Quality Compounders)
These companies demonstrate strong, consistent growth—often thanks to competitive advantages and market leadership:

- UnitedHealth Group (UNH): A diversified healthcare firm offering insurance and medical services.

- Costco Wholesale Corporation (COST): A membership-based wholesale retailer known for customer loyalty and operational efficiency.

- Thermo Fisher Scientific (TMO): A provider of laboratory equipment and services, benefiting from growth in scientific research.

Stocks with 20%+ CAGR (Exceptional Growth Stories) These companies have delivered outstanding growth, often by disrupting entire industries or capitalizing on emerging trends:

- NVIDIA Corporation (NVDA): A leader in graphics processing units (GPUs), benefiting from trends in gaming, AI, and data centers.

- Tesla Inc. (TSLA): An electric vehicle and clean energy company that has rapidly expanded its market presence.

- ASML Holding N.V. (ASML): A crucial supplier of photolithography systems for the semiconductor industry, essential to chip manufacturing.

Note: The CAGR figures are estimates based on historical performance over the past ten years (as of 2025) and are subject to market fluctuations. For simplicity, these figures assume reinvestment and do not account for taxes.

Three Key Takeaways:

- Time matters more than timing. The longer you stay invested in a great company, the less starting capital you need.

- Returns matter— but starting early is just as crucial. Even 15% per year can significantly grow modest capital over a decade.

- This leads to a familiar but wise insight: *Most people overestimate what they can accomplish in a year and underestimate what they can achieve in ten.* A one-stock portfolio capitalizes on exactly that advantage.

And remember: If you're starting small, don't rush—give yourself time. Big things take time. Time is on your side—if you let the power of compounding work for you.

Profiting from Stock Trends with Long-Term Options

It's well known that building wealth in the stock market can also be faster or more cost-efficient—there are plenty of tools for that. I explain in detail how to build wealth with leveraged products in my book *How to Turn $5,000 into a Million*. If you're interested in those strategies, you might want to check it out. But here, the focus is on the idea of using a single stock—or a single focused idea—to make the leap to wealth. If you have limited capital or only want to risk a small amount, it's worth looking into long-term options, also known as LEAPS.

Long-term options are call or put options with maturities ranging from 12 months to several years. Unlike short-term options, which often expire within a few weeks or months, LEAPS provide more time for the stock to move as anticipated. They allow investors to participate in a stock's price development with less capital, since buying an option is generally cheaper than buying the underlying stock. The key features of long-term options are:

- Leverage: With a relatively small capital outlay, an investor can gain exposure to the price movement of a stock.

- Time value: Thanks to the longer maturity, the rate of time decay (theta) is lower than with short-term options.

- Flexibility: Investors can speculate on both rising prices (with calls) and falling prices (with puts).

Why should an investor consider using long-term options for medium-term strategies?

Medium-term price movements—typically over 6 to 24 months—are often driven by broader trends like company developments, sector cycles, or macroeconomic changes. LEAPS are well-suited for taking advantage of such trends because they provide enough time for the market to reflect the expected move. They are also cost-effective: you can control a larger position with less capital, and the maximum loss is limited to the option premium paid. Here are some common strategies for using long-term options to benefit from medium-term price trends:

1. Buying Call Options for Bullish Outlooks

If you expect a stock to rise in value over the medium term, you can buy a call option. This strategy is especially useful if the stock seems too expensive to buy outright, but you still want to benefit from a price increase.

Example: Stock XYZ is trading at $100. You expect it to rise to $150 within 18 months. You buy a LEAPS call option with a strike price of $110 for $10 (the premium).

If the stock rises to $150, the option is "in the money" and has an intrinsic value of $40 ($150 − $110).

Your profit is $30 per option (excluding fees), which corresponds to a 300% return.

The advantage is clear: You have the potential for a high return with low capital investment, while your risk is limited. If the stock doesn't perform as expected, the option expires worthless, and you lose only the premium.

2. Stock Replacement Strategy

Instead of buying shares outright, investors can purchase long-term in-the-money (ITM) call options—those with a strike price below the current market price. These options typically have a high delta (close to 1), meaning they move almost one-to-one with the underlying stock but require far less capital.

Example:

Stock XYZ is trading at $100. Instead of buying 100 shares for $10,000, you purchase a long-term ITM LEAPS call with a strike price of $80 for $25 per share (total cost: $2,500 for control over 100 shares).

If the stock rises to $130, the option will be worth approximately $50 ($130 – $80), giving you a gain of $25 per share.

The advantage is clear: you use less capital and your risk is limited—to the option premium and potential volatility shifts.

Important Considerations When Using Long-Term Options

Using long-dated options requires caution and competence. You must be able to evaluate the quality and potential price development of the stock. Understanding volatility is also essential, since implied volatility affects the option premium.

High volatility increases the cost but can also create larger profit potential. Also, pay attention to option liquidity—choose contracts with sufficient trading volume to ensure tight bid-ask spreads and smooth execution.

As always, consistent risk management is essential—only invest capital you can afford to lose. Despite their benefits, long-term options are not risk-free. If the stock does not perform as expected, the option can expire worthless. There's also time decay to consider: while LEAPS lose value more slowly than short-term options, time decay accelerates as expiration nears.

3. Rolling LEAPS: Extending a Position in Long-Term Trends

LEAPS eventually expire. If the trend is still intact when expiration approaches, you likely don't want to exit—you want to extend. This is where *rolling* comes in: you sell your current call option (before it expires) and buy a new one, typically with a later expiration and potentially a higher strike price. This lets you lock in gains, reset the clock, and stay engaged in the position.

Example:

In 2023, you buy a call option on Apple expiring in January 2025 with a $300 strike for $40. By the end of 2024, it's worth $90. You sell the option and realize your gain. Then you purchase a new call expiring in January 2027 with a $400 strike price for $50. You've now rolled the position forward and continue to bet on Apple's growth.

Rolling allows long-term LEAPS traders to stay with multi-year megatrends, even when individual options expire.

LEAPS extend your participation in these trends. They let you gradually raise strike prices as the stock rises, locking in gains while maintaining exposure. LEAPS also smooth out volatility, and by rolling regularly, you avoid watching an option expire worthless. Rolling LEAPS is like reloading your cannon every year or two—without losing sight of the target.

Applying This in a One-Stock Portfolio

Let's say you believe in Nvidia, Tesla, or Apple for the next ten years. You can buy 2-year LEAPS aligned with your target stock's growth. Size your positions carefully—remember that options can expire worthless. Track performance and implied volatility. Roll into new LEAPS six to twelve months before expiration, or earlier if the stock has moved significantly and your current option is deep in the money. Repeat every one to two years as long as the trend remains intact.

However, do *not* overleverage—just because one contract gives you exposure to 100 shares doesn't mean you should overextend yourself. Don't wait too long to roll, as time decay accelerates close to expiration. Most importantly, don't buy LEAPS on low-quality stocks. Focus on high-conviction, high-quality trend stocks and use deep-in-the-money calls for a more secure approach.

Why Bitcoin Might Be a Strong Candidate for a One-Stock Portfolio

A one-stock portfolio is about identifying a unique, asymmetric idea with the potential to create wealth far beyond the ordinary. For many investors, this might be a company like Apple, Amazon, or Nvidia. But for an increasing number of visionary thinkers, the best "stock" to own isn't a company at all — it's Bitcoin.

In this chapter, I want to explore why Bitcoin, though not a traditional company, could be an excellent candidate for a concentrated, long-term investment — and why it shares many of the core traits of a compound interest engine. This is, of course, not investment advice; every investor should independently research this cryptocurrency before making a decision. Bitcoin is not a company — it is a protocol. And that is precisely its strength. Bitcoin has no CEO, no earnings reports, no quarterly results. It has no marketing team, no headquarters, no human resources department.

What Bitcoin offers instead: immutable code, a predetermined cap of 21 million coins, global acceptance, decentralized control, and a market that runs 24/7. In other words: Bitcoin is the purest asset ever invented. It is independent of politics, immune to inflation, and secured by mathematics instead of trust. While companies can be disrupted, taxed, or poorly managed, Bitcoin simply continues operating. That is not a weakness — it's the foundation of its *antifragility*.

The best companies have wide moats. These typically consist of:

- Brand power (Apple)
- Network effects (Meta)
- Technological superiority (Nvidia)

What is Bitcoin's moat?

Bitcoin's core advantage is *mathematical scarcity*. There will never be more than 21 million Bitcoins. The issuance schedule is fixed and predictable. No CEO, central bank, or government can alter that. This hard cap represents the ultimate form of scarcity — a property no fiat currency or corporate equity can replicate. In a world of endless monetary expansion, Bitcoin stands as a fortress of finite supply.

Bitcoin's version of compound interest takes a different form: price plus adoption. It pays no dividends, executes no buybacks, and doesn't grow profits. Yet it compounds in two ways:

1. Price appreciation, driven by scarcity and demand
2. Network expansion, as more and more people around the world adopt Bitcoin

In other words: Every new user strengthens the network. Every new holder reduces the circulating supply. Every halving cuts new issuance. Every institution, nation, or company adopting

Bitcoin increases its perceived legitimacy. This creates a self-reinforcing cycle — the very definition of compound interest.

Bitcoin's performance speaks for itself. Let's look at the numbers: Over the past ten years (2013–2023), Bitcoin achieved an average annual growth rate (CAGR) of over 50%. That outpaces the S&P 500, the Nasdaq, gold, and virtually every other major asset. Despite multiple corrections of 70–80%, the long-term trend has remained explosive. Bitcoin rewards patience, foresight, and discipline — precisely the traits needed for a one-stock portfolio.

What about volatility? Yes, Bitcoin is volatile — no question about it. As an investor, you should occasionally expect drawdowns of more than 50%. At the same time, bull markets with gains of over 600% are also part of the picture. Volatility is not the real risk. The real risk is the permanent loss of your coins. For long-term investors, volatility is just noise. Let's take a look at the long-term Bitcoin chart.

Chart 23: Bitcoin, 2011–2025, Monthly Chart, Logarithmic Scale

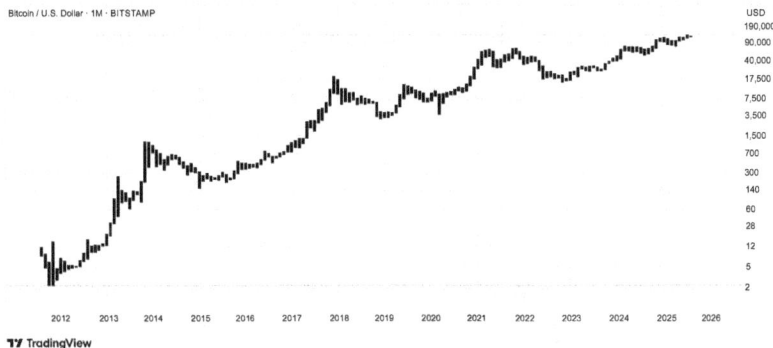

Bitcoin / U.S. Dollar · 1M · BITSTAMP

USD
190,000
90,000
40,000
17,500
7,500
3,500
1,500
700
300
140
60
28
12
5
2

2012   2013   2014   2015   2016   2017   2018   2019   2020   2021   2022   2023   2024   2025   2026

TradingView

Volatility is the price of unprecedented upside potential and the possibility of a fundamental transformation of the global monetary system. By the way: Amazon, Tesla, and Nvidia were — and still are — volatile as well. If you can't handle Bitcoin's volatility, you don't deserve its compounding effect.

Now let's compare Bitcoin to the characteristics of a strong stock candidate:

- Durable competitive advantage: Yes – Fixed supply and decentralization
- High return on value: Yes – Price appreciation over time
- Visionary founder: Yes – Satoshi created it and then stepped away
- Option value / future potential: Yes – Global reserve currency, L2 apps, ETFs
- Long-term growth potential: Yes – Still early in the adoption curve
- Resilience to macro and market shocks: Yes – Has survived every crash and continues to grow

So how can Bitcoin be considered a "stock"? While it isn't a company, Bitcoin behaves like a self-growing digital organism — a monetary startup with no CEO. It's a network-effect business, much like the Internet itself. Within a one-stock portfolio, Bitcoin might be the purest expression of uncorrelated, asymmetric returns and truly global scalability, with an antifragile design.

For those new to cryptocurrency, the following section provides an overview of different ways to invest in Bitcoin or other crypto assets.

1. Direct Ownership (Buying and Holding Real Bitcoins)

Best suited for investors with long-term conviction who want full control. You buy actual Bitcoin (BTC) and store it in a digital wallet. To do this, you open an account with a crypto exchange (e.g., Coinbase, Kraken, Bitpanda), purchase BTC, and transfer it to a hardware wallet like Ledger or Trezor (for cold storage).

Advantages: You own the Bitcoin directly and store your coins offline (based on the principle "Not your keys, not your coins"). There is no third-party risk if you self-custody.

Disadvantages: You are fully responsible for the security of your coins. Offline storage reduces liquidity.

2. Bitcoin ETFs (Spot- or Futures-Based)

Best suited for traditional investors who want exposure through brokerage accounts. You don't own actual Bitcoin, but a regulated fund that tracks BTC's price. Examples:

- Spot ETFs (e.g., BlackRock iShares Bitcoin Trust, Fidelity Wise Origin)

- Futures ETFs (e.g., ProShares BITO): Use CME futures to simulate BTC exposure.

Advantages:

- Easy to buy through regular brokerage accounts

- No wallet or key management required

- Held and regulated by institutions

- Eligible for tax-advantaged accounts (e.g., IRA, 401(k), ETF wrappers)

Disadvantages:

- You don't own real Bitcoin
- ETF fees can reduce returns
- No usability (e.g., you can't move or spend BTC)

3. Bitcoin Derivatives (Options, Futures)

Ideal for active traders with high risk tolerance. You trade contracts that reflect the price of Bitcoin, with or without leverage. Platforms include Deribit, Binance, CME (for futures), or Bybit. You can trade options or perpetual futures. These instruments offer high leverage potential and can be used for hedging, speculation, or generating returns. You can also benefit from short-term moves and volatility.

Disadvantages: Crypto futures are risky and not suitable for long-term investments. You never actually own Bitcoin — just its derivatives.

4. Bitcoin Mining Stocks or Funds

Indirect exposure via companies active in the Bitcoin ecosystem. You invest in firms that mine Bitcoin or support its infrastructure. Examples:

- Riot Platforms (RIOT)
- Marathon Digital Holdings (MARA)
- Bitfarms, CleanSpark, etc.

You benefit from potential upside in BTC prices and operational leverage. These investments are tradable through equity accounts and often offer higher beta relative to BTC.

Disadvantages: Business risks exist (e.g., energy costs, dilution, regulation). These stocks are more volatile than BTC itself, and you don't own any real Bitcoin.

5. Crypto-Based Yield Platforms (Lending Out Your BTC)

Suited for advanced users seeking passive income. You deposit BTC to earn interest or use it as collateral.

Platforms: Binance Earn, Nexo, Ledn, etc.

You can earn passive returns (e.g., 1–4% APY) and access loans without selling BTC.

Disadvantages:

- Counterparty risk (platform bankruptcy — e.g., Celsius, BlockFi)
- Not ideal for large holdings
- Often better avoided by long-term holders

6. Bitcoin in Retirement Accounts or Tax-Advantaged Accounts

Ideal for investors based in the U.S. or EU with long-term financial planning goals. You hold Bitcoin in a tax-advantaged environment.

- Use self-directed IRAs (e.g., IRAtrust, Alto IRA)
- Or purchase spot Bitcoin ETFs in your standard retirement or pension plan.

Advantages:

- Long-term capital gains are shielded or deferred

- Ideal for wealth preservation and estate planning

Disadvantages:

- Often limited flexibility with assets (no self-custody)

- Some providers charge higher fees

7. Strategy (MSTR) – A Compelling Alternative to Direct Bitcoin Ownership

Strategy (formerly MicroStrategy) is no longer a typical software company – it has effectively transformed into a publicly traded Bitcoin holding fund. As of May 2025, Strategy holds over 576,000 bitcoins, financed through equity, profits, and debt. Because Strategy has taken on debt to acquire Bitcoin, investors gain implicit leverage on Bitcoin's price – without personally using leverage. When Bitcoin rises, MSTR often rises disproportionately.

The advantage of buying Strategy: You can purchase MSTR stock directly through your brokerage account, without needing to handle wallets, private keys, or crypto exchanges. In some countries, buying stock may offer tax advantages over buying cryptocurrency directly, depending on holding period and account structure.

That said, Strategy is a kind of "Bitcoin on steroids" – a publicly traded vehicle to participate in the Bitcoin boom, with added leverage and institutional access. It's ideal for investors who are bullish on Bitcoin but prefer to use the traditional stock market to invest.

Summary: Choose What Fits You

- If you believe in Bitcoin as digital gold: own the original and store it securely.

- If you prefer simplicity and structure: buy a spot ETF in your brokerage account.

- If you want to trade momentum: use LEAPS, futures, or options.

- If you want to build wealth long-term in a tax-efficient way: use Bitcoin ETFs in retirement accounts.

- If you want to enhance returns or speculate: consider mining stocks or buying Strategy (MSTR).

There is no one-size-fits-all approach to Bitcoin or cryptocurrency. The best form of Bitcoin exposure is the one that aligns with your goals, risk tolerance, and time horizon.

Afterword

Dear reader, With this book, I have taken you on a journey— one centered around an idea as simple as it is powerful: the conviction that a single investment in a single asset can be enough to build lasting wealth. If you take this idea seriously and follow it through to its logical conclusion, you almost inevitably arrive at the considerations I've shared with you here.

Some may find this concept appealing. For others, it might seem daring—or even absurd: to put all your eggs in one basket. But regardless of how you choose to act after reading this book, you won't be able to avoid one essential question—a question every serious investor must face sooner or later: *How large should each position in your portfolio be?*

Oddly, this is a topic rarely discussed in the world of investing. People obsess over *what* to buy—that's the domain of fundamental analysis. They argue about *when* to buy—that's where technical analysis comes in. But the question of *how much?* That's often neglected, even though it can be the deciding factor between a good trade and a life-changing outcome.

This book is my attempt to place the question of "how much" at the center of the conversation—or, more precisely: how large a position needs to be to actually make a meaningful impact.

Because once you've found a real winner in your portfolio, it's only logical to want as much of it as possible.

Look at the stories of well-known—and lesser-known—successful investors. Of course, choosing the right stock mattered. Timing played a role too. But what made the real difference, almost every time, was the *size* of the position. Whether someone managed to build real wealth didn't primarily depend on whether they had a brilliant analysis or perfect timing—but on how decisively they bet on their conviction.

The case studies in this book make that clear: these people didn't become wealthy because they had ten good ideas. They became wealthy because they made one big bet. They didn't spread their capital thin across many opportunities. They concentrated it—boldly—on what they believed in. The size of the position was the lever that turned a successful investment into a transformative one.

Of course, that takes courage, conviction—and often a fair amount of nerve. But that's exactly why I wrote this book: to challenge you to think differently. Not just about what you buy. Not just about when you buy it. But about the thing that is almost never discussed, even though it may be the most important factor of all: **How much you buy.** Because in the end, it is often not the content of an idea, but the intensity with which it is pursued, that determines the outcome.

Glossary

Average Cost Effect: The average return achieved through regular investing compared to a lump-sum investment.

Broker: A financial service provider responsible for executing securities orders.

Brokerage Account: A securities account where an investor manages their investments.

CAGR: Compound Annual Growth Rate – the average annual growth rate of an investment over a specified period, accounting for compounding.

Cash Flow: A financial metric comparing inflows and outflows of cash over a specific period.

Churn Rate: The rate at which customers stop doing business with a company.

Compound Interest Effect: Interest added to the principal, which then earns interest itself over time.

Consumer Goods: Products made for personal use or consumption.

Cost Leadership: A business strategy aiming to achieve a competitive edge through lower production costs.

Customer Lifetime Value (CLV): The total value a customer contributes to a company over the entire duration of the relationship.

Diversification: The practice of spreading investments across different assets to reduce risk.

Dividend: A portion of a company's profits paid out to shareholders.

Dollar Cost Averaging: The practice of investing fixed amounts regularly, regardless of market price, to reduce the impact of volatility.

Drawdown: A decline in the value of a portfolio or asset from its peak over a specific period.

Economies of Scale: Cost advantages achieved as production scales, leading to lower per-unit costs.

Efficient Market Hypothesis: The theory that markets fully reflect all available information, making it impossible to consistently outperform..

ETF: Exchange-Traded Fund – an investment fund traded on stock exchanges like a stock.

Exponential Growth: A growth pattern where values increase by the same proportion in equal time intervals.

Fiat Currency: Government-issued currency not backed by a physical commodity like gold or silver.

Financial Crisis: The global banking and economic crisis that began in 2007.

Flywheel Effect: Companies harness customer satisfaction to drive referrals and repeat purchases.

Fundamentals: Key financial metrics and indicators of a company's performance.

Futures: Standardized contracts to buy or sell an asset at a predetermined price and date in the future.

Hedging: Financial strategies to protect against risk, such as price or currency fluctuations.

Index: A basket of assets like stocks or bonds used to track the performance of a specific sector or market.

LEAPS: Long-Term Equity Anticipation Securities – options with extended expiration dates, often over a year.

Leasehold: Long-term land use, typically over 50 to 99 years

Leverage Effect: Using borrowed capital to increase the return on equity.

Lock-In Effect: High customer retention due to switching costs or barriers.

Loss of Purchasing Power: Inflation or sustained price increases that reduce the value of money.

Magnificent Seven: A group of seven major tech firms – Apple, Microsoft, Amazon, Alphabet, Meta, Nvidia, and Tesla.

Margin: Collateral required from an investor to enter a futures position.

Margin Account: A brokerage account allowing the use of leverage to buy securities.

Margin Compression: Occurs when the gap between sales and production costs narrows significantly.

Moat: A quality of businesses that enjoy sustainable competitive advantages protecting them from rivals.

Market Capitalization: The total market value of a company's outstanding shares.

MSCI World: A global index tracking the equity performance of 1,500 companies in 23 developed countries.

Misallocation: Inefficient or inappropriate distribution of capital or resources.

Online Broker: A brokerage offering trading services exclusively online.

Option: A financial contract giving the right, but not the obligation, to buy or sell an asset at a predetermined price.

Penny Stocks: Low-priced stocks, often under five dollars per share, typically from small-cap companies.

Portfolio: The full collection of assets held by an investor.

Portfolio Theory: A field of finance studying investment behavior and asset allocation.

Private Equity: Investments in privately held, non-public companies.

Recency Bias: A cognitive bias where recent events are given greater importance than historical ones.

Return on Equity (ROE): A measure of profitability indicating how effectively a company uses shareholders' equity

Return on Invested Capital (ROIC): A measure of how efficiently a company uses capital to generate returns.

Return on Capital: A metric used to evaluate the profitability of an investment relative to capital employed.

S&P 500: A stock market index of 500 leading publicly traded U.S. companies.

Startup: A new company with an innovative business idea and high growth potential.

Stock Index: A metric representing the performance of the overall stock market or specific groups of stocks

Stock Portfolio: The entirety of an investor's equity investments.

Stock Replacement: An options strategy mimicking stock ownership with less capital commitment.

Stock Split: A corporate action that increases the number of shares while keeping the company's market capitalization unchanged.

Track Record: A history of performance for a person, company, or product.

Underperformer: A stock that fails to meet performance expectations.

Vertical Integration: When a company controls multiple stages of its supply chain.

Volatility: A measure of price fluctuations; typically expressed as standard deviation.

Wu Wei: A core Taoist concept advocating effortless action in harmony with nature.

Other Books by Heikin Ashi Trader

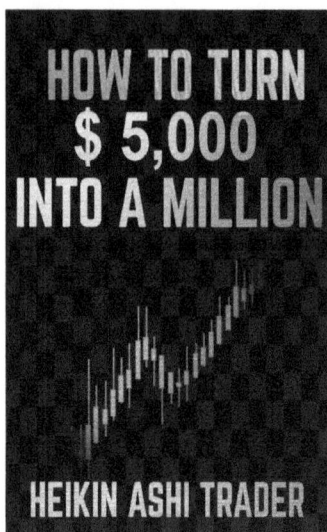

How to Turn $ 5,000 into a Million

Can you become a millionaire on the stock market? The question of how to grow a small account undoubtedly occupies every trader's mind. How do you manage to make a fortune out of a small amount? And preferably really fast?

Just as it is possible to build a real estate empire without a dollar of equity, so it is also possible to achieve high profits on the stock market with a small amount of starting capital (USD 5000 or less).

In this book, Heikin Ashi Trader presents a stock market strategy that will help the trader to succeed in this endeavor. Above all, he explains that the factor of position size plays a much more decisive role in trading success than is commonly assumed. The right question is not: how often are you right or wrong, but how big is your position if you are right?

This method is just about finding the markets where a significant movement can be expected. And once he has identified one, the trader should build a big position in that market, so that he can fully benefit from this movement.

Table of Contents

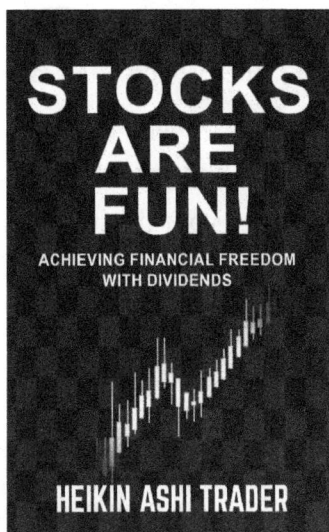

Stocks are fun!

Achieving financial freedom with dividends

Earlier generations invested in stocks because they had an income that never ran dry. In contrast to investors, who bet on price increases, wealthy people of all ages buy dividend stocks, and they consistently reinvest either the regular distributions, or they use them as income in their old age.

In this first part of the series of books on stocks, the author shows how investing in dividend stocks can, over time, lead to a significant accumulation of wealth that an individual can live on for decades, even in old age.

Building wealth does not have to be boring. In fact, it can even be a lot of fun. If you observe how your shares pay you dividends every month, you stay motivated and continue to invest. Moreover, you do not even need starting capital to get going. Even investors with little money can build up significant assets in the age of online brokers. The author shows exactly how to do this in a separate chapter, in which he uses true-to-life examples to explain how much you need to save every month, in order to achieve your financial goals.

Table of contents

Part 1: If it is not fun, you will not hold out

Why shares are fun!

Why you should become an income investor

Why dividend income offers more security than your job

What you need most when you get older: A regular income!

Why you need to understand the term "cash flow" if you want to become financially independent

Why your bank advisor does not recommend that you become an income investor

As an income investor you are (and remain) involved in economic life

Part 2: Introduction to the World of Dividends

What are dividends?

Why do companies pay dividends?

When will the dividends be paid?

What is the dividend yield?

What is the payout ratio (dividend payout ratio)?

Why should you invest in dividend stocks?

Ordinary people who have become millionaires, thanks to dividends

Example 1: Anne Scheiber

Example 2: Ronald Read

Example 3: Grace Groner

What is the compound interest effect?

High dividends or dividend growth?

Which sectors pay the highest dividends?

Part 3: How do I prepare for income investment?

How much should I save?

How do I set up a Watchlist?

What shares does Warren Buffett buy?

Why I prefer American stocks

Who are the dividend kings?

How to open a broker account?

What is the security identification number?

Which dividend shares should I buy now?

How does the Dollar Cost Average Method work?

What is a dividend reinvestment plan (DRIP)?

Why monthly payers are interesting

How often should I check my shares?

What to do if the stock market crashes?

About the Author

Heikin Ashi Trader is the pseudonym of a trader with over 24 years of experience in day trading futures and currencies. After working for a hedge fund, he became an independent trader. He specializes in scalping and short-term day trading. His book *Scalping Is Fun!* became an international bestseller, selling over 50,000 copies and translated into 11 languages. He has also published numerous other trading books that build upon and complement one another in content. More information can be found at: www.heikinashitrader.net